THEORETICAL ETHICS

BY

MILTON VALENTINE, D.D., LL. D.

Ex-President of Pennsylvania College, and Professor of
Theology
in the Lutheran Theological Seminary, Gettysburg, Pa.,
Author of "Natural Theology or Rational Theism"

Just
SINNER

www.JustandSinner.com

THEORETICAL ETHICS BY MILTON VALENTINE

Permission inquiries may be sent to
JustandSinner@yahoo.com

Just & Sinner
1467 Walnut Ave.
Brighton, IA 52540

www.JustandSinner.com

ISBN 10: **0692261613**
ISBN 13: **978-0692261613**

Original Publishing Info:
CHICAGO
SCOTT, FORESMAN & CO.
1897
Copyright, 1897, by
SCOTT, FORESMAN & Co.

PREFACE

ETHICAL Theory has felt the full force of recent scientific and philosophical agitation. The earlier systems have been subject to earnest and continued discussion. The severest tests available by the progress of knowledge have been applied to both their premises and their conclusions. New theories, based on changed conceptions of man and the world, have been variously elaborated, presenting greatly altered views of the whole phenomenon of morality. While not overthrowing old views these have given instructive suggestions. The ethical field has thus been largely re-surveyed, and whatever light modern science and speculation have furnished has been thrown upon this great and unceasingly important subject. In some respects the agitation has brought confusion and uncertainty. The clash of theories has been disturbing. But on the whole ethical philosophy has been the gainer. The discussions have certified the immovable foundations and essential features of the moral system. The fresh light from the advance of knowledge has proved, as it always does, not destructive, but corrective and confirmatory. The abiding truth has been shown and vindicated by the ordeal through which it has passed.

This volume is largely the outcome of the author's many years of class-room lecturing on the subject. Its object is to furnish for students and general readers a compendious view of the ethical facts and principles as the author believes them to be established by the best accredited knowledge and thought of our times. There seems to be room for such a work. The method is believed to give proper recognition to both the empirical and metaphysical sides of the subject. Starting from the universal phenomenon of moral distinctions in life, it determines the conscience psychologically, as a rationally intuitive power discerning the moral distinction and the reality and authority of moral law. The implications of conscience and moral law necessarily become theistic. The metaphysical examination finds for the real phenomena of the subjective faculty the objective and abiding reality of the ethical law which the faculty discerns, and the right or morally good itself so perceived as consisting proximately in a conformity of conduct with the relations of life in which moral requirement meets human freedom, and as ultimately grounded in the absolute and perfect source of the moral constitution of the universe. The movement carries to the conclusion of eternal and immutable moral law. The disclosures of revelation confirm the ethical law of the natural reason, completing the moral view and supplying, in the divine forces of Christianity, the proper dynamic for the realization of the ethical life.

The volume is humbly sent forth in the hope that it may contribute somewhat to the cause of truth and prove quickening to the life of duty and righteousness.

GETTYSBURG, Dec. 1, 1896.

CONTENTS

CHAPTER I
DEFINITION AND GENERAL DIVISIONS...9

CHAPTER II
THE FACT OF MORAL DISTINCTIONS...19

CHAPTER III
FACULTY OF MORAL DISTINCTIONS—THE EXISTENCE OF CONSCIENCE...27

CHAPTER IV
THE FACULTY OF MORAL DISTINCTIONS—THE NATURE OF CONSCIENCE...41

CHAPTER V
THE SUPREMACY OF CONSCIENCE...63

CHAPTER VI
MORAL AGENCY...73

CHAPTER VII
THE REALITY OF RIGHT AND WRONG...87

CHAPTER VIII
THE GROUND OF RIGHT...101

CHAPTER IX
THE GROUND OF RIGHT—CONTINUED...123

CHAPTER X
THE OBJECTS OF THE MORAL JUDGMENT...135

CHAPTER XI
THE ETHICAL VIEW UNDER CHRISTIAN TEACHING...147

CHAPTER XII
THE ETHICAL TASK UNDER CHRISTIANITY...163

CHAPTER 1

DEFINITION AND DIVISIONS
Ethics Defined

1. Ethics is the science of rectitude and duty. It treats of the right and its obligations. Its subject is morality. Its sphere is the sphere of virtuous conduct. It covers a double range of inquiry, as the subject-matter lies within or without the human constitution. On the one side it investigates and sets forth the facts and laws of man's moral constitution; on the other, the nature and grounds of the distinction of right and wrong. In the light of the whole investigation into these fundamental verities, it determines the principles and rules of duty in the various relations of life. It thus discovers and elucidates the underlying pre-suppositions and principles upon which the phenomena of moral discernment and obligation rest, and on which man rises into the possibility and reality of character, as his supreme distinction among the orders of existence on earth. The inquiry throughout is conducted according to the scientific method of careful observation and analysis of the unquestionable facts concerned, and an orderly presentation of their necessary logical implications and conclusions. Hence the product of the investigation, as the systematized view of the facts, with their underlying principles, may justly be called, as it usually is called, moral science.

The term Ethics, which we thus use to designate this branch of study, with its systematized truth, is not employed with etymological strictness. For it comes from the Greek ἦθος, moral character, which, according to Aristotle is derived from ἔθος, custom, under the notion that moral virtue is a product of repeated acts of voluntary preference. Taken strictly this would build rectitude or the ethically right on the mere habits or usages of a people. But this conception of the basis of virtue must not be included and carried into the scientific use of the word, or be at all allowed to prejudice the final decision of this great question of the foundation of right, in the end, in the light of all the facts in the case.

The Latin equivalent for ἦθος was *mos*, with similar suggestion as to the nature of rectitude, and human duty was treated under the head of De Moribus. Cicero says: "*Quia pertinet ad mores, quod ἦθος illi vocant, nos eam partem philosophiæ De Moribus appellare solemus; sed decet augentem linguam Latinam nominare Moralem.*" This suggestion of Cicero has given the common English designation Morals or Moral Philosophy. Recent usage, however, speaks of the study rather as moral science, in harmony with the prevailing preference for the term science in all investigations conducted under the inductive method. It is, nevertheless, as will appear, largely a metaphysical and philosophical investigation, and, if classed as science, must be counted as pre-eminently a philosophical science.

Historical Glance

2. The beginning of the movement to give a systematic view of ethical truth may be traced to Socrates. The pre-Socratic philosophy failed to produce anything that can be called a system in this connection. The difficulty in the way was not only the want of a scientific spirit at that period, but especially the inadequate and false light in which human beings were viewed. Outside of the Hebrew people there was little or no recognition of the freedom of man, as man. Such freedom was denied both in thought and in life. Everywhere, in India, China, and Egypt, as well as in Greece and Rome, the immense mass of the population were in a condition of abject slavery, regarded as chattels, not amenable to the responsibilities of moral life. Only the free citizens were viewed as capable of virtue. Slavery was a part of the very conception of the State. The essential characteristics and rights of humanity were not thought of as belonging to all men. But moral life, as will appear, can exist only in the sphere of liberty. Even the most advanced philosophers of the ancient

world extended the conception of moral manhood only to the free citizen, the status of the rest not bringing them within the possibility of even civic virtue. And even the so-called free citizen existed almost absolutely for the State. His sacred selfhood disappeared under ownership by the Government, by which he was held and used as a machine for military service. Even long after Socrates opened the way, within this limited range, toward some connected view of ethical life, these disabling causes continued to distort and impede all efforts to systematize the principles which underlie and determine it. Plato, Aristotle, and the philosophers generally, continued to know nothing of a morality for all human beings.

It is to be remembered, too, that this tardy appearance of effort in scientific ethics is part of the wider fact, that in that period of human history even the most advanced tribes and nations had not risen to science at all. All knowledge was in the non-scientific form, or only fragmentarily and inchoately adjusted. The moral consciousness and personal virtues, however, of course existed, as part of the normal constitution and practical activities of human life. The various peoples had collections of moral precepts and rules for right living, often bright with gems of ethical truth and beauty, usually in close connection with religious beliefs and convictions; but these were not based and unified on any underlying principles bringing them logically into compact and consistent system. Just as the facts and practices of religion existed, in even rich luxuriance, anterior to the appearance of speculative theologies, and the phenomena of nature for long centuries preceded the formation of the natural sciences, so the moral constitution of the race and practical morality existed long in advance of the explanations and systemization that create the science of ethics.

The history of the science does not come within the purpose of this work. The greatness of the speculative and practical questions involved in the subject, clearly and impressively apparent when once brought forward, could not fail to awaken and hold the most earnest interest of the human mind. They concerned the powers and possibilities of man in the crowning endowments of his nature, and in the highest ascent of their evident intention and adaptation. They touched the great problems of personal and social welfare in the most vital relations and decisive interests. So the old sages became moralists and their great themes were the themes of virtue and duty. Not very deeply, however, did they, for centuries, succeed in penetrating the rational principles of the moral life and the authority of the moral judgments. Yet clear gems of thought and deep suggestion mark the pathway of their thinking. In passing on, and over from pagan into Christian development, the treatment was mostly in connection with religious truths, and as involved in theological doctrine. In the light of the Christian Scriptures the whole subject came under a new illumination. The various duties, however, in the different relations of life, were permitted to rest, without much theorizing, on the warrant of supernatural revelation and divine precept. Down through the early Christian period, and the centuries of medieval scholasticism, and on through the Renaissance and the Reformation and the subsequent dogmatic period of Protestant theology, ethics continued to be treated simply as a division of theology, based almost wholly on the Sacred Scriptures, with but little inclusion of any effort to determine its natural basis and significance. But with the age of modern philosophy and science a new interest and direction came to ethical inquiry. Explanation began to be sought for the unique authority of the ethical judgments, and concerning the place of the moral power in the essential constitution of the human soul. Special emphasis was given to the fact that, even apart from the precepts of revelation, man is bound to rectitude by an imperative within him, which is not of his choice, but claims the right to dominate his choices. And since the seventeenth century the ethical constitution of humanity, together with the nature and grounds of right, has been made, apart from theology, the distinct and separate theme of scientific and philosophical investigation and discussion. It has been among the leading subjects of rational inquiry and constructive effort. Especially in Great Britain and in our own country has the inquiry been conducted on this basis, and directed to the exhibition of the natural foundation and character of the ethical distinctions and judgments, and to a systemization of the ethical realities and laws thus determinable.

The work thus done has created an immense literature, and established a body of securely authenticated scientific results.

3. Ethics, in its comprehensive sense, is naturally divided into two leading parts—Theoretical Ethics, and Practical or Applied Ethics.

Theoretical Ethics

(1) Theoretical Ethics deals with the essential realities and principles which form the fundamental basis and source of obligation and moral law, in the constitution of man and of the world. It is a speculative study, seeking a rational account of the foundations of morality and behests of duty. It secures a theory from and of the facts. It has, however, a double range of investigation, as it seeks to determine the truth with respect to the two great essential factors in the aggregate inquiry.

In the one range it examines and ascertains the facts and laws of man's moral nature. It investigates the constitution of the moral agent, in whose conscious experience, in the presence of the concrete world, the moral phenomena arise. In this part, the inquiry is psychological, and its results are scientific.

In the other range it investigates the nature and ground of right, or the morally good. In this the search is not for what is discoverable within the moral agent, or the phenomena of the moral perceptions and emotions, but for that which is without him and to which his moral life is, at least apparently, required to be adjusted. Here the work is metaphysical, passing on from what is phenomenal within man, and looking for the super-phenomenal realities implied. The process and results here are philosophical.

It thus appears that the one range of investigation moves subjectively, the other objectively. The first discovers what man is—at least so far as his constitution embraces those powers, perceptions, judgments and feelings in which he becomes and recognizes himself a moral being; the second seeks to know what rectitude is, or what is that to which the moral perceptions and discriminations refer and bind. When the truth on both these sides is discovered and brought together, the whole view, with

13

the particulars logically correlated, will present the aggregate theory of duty, or the rationale of obligation.

Practical Ethics

(2) Practical Ethics sets forth the proper application of these fundamental principles of right and duty, as developed and justified in theoretical ethics, to the varied relations of men, personally, in the Family, in Society, and in the State. It passes on from the philosophy of moral obligations to a settlement of particular duties in the different spheres of human life and activity.

The connection between theoretical and practical ethics is very close and vital. Theory and practice always affect each other. They cannot be held wholly apart. They act and react on each other, in ceaseless influences. It is so in every department of thought and life. Theoretical error in physical science, in art, in trade, in political economy, can hardly fail to appear in faulty or misdirected practice. Every failure to grasp first principles correctly and firmly is sure to mean failure also to grasp and maintain the true order and beauty of right living. False views as to the reality and grounds of moral obligation weaken, vitiate and corrupt life. They become, often, the fountain of far-flowing streams of evil and blight. At best they lack power for the true and right life. A correct theory of ethical truth is, therefore, demanded by all the high interests in the moral life of man and the order of the world.

It is apparent, however, that it is only the theoretical part that constitutes the science of ethics. It alone settles the systematic view of it, revealing its underlying pre-suppositions and principles, exhibiting its reasons and determining its laws. Practical ethics, as simply pointing out how these bear upon men's temper and conduct in actual life, is apart from the scientific investigation. Though this has usually constituted a large portion of formal treatises on the subject, we, for the reason thus given, omit it from this discussion.

4. A few of the relations of ethical science are properly called to mind here. Its place will thus be more clearly seen. It sustains very close relations to three other great branches of study.

Relation to Psychology

(1) To psychology. It is organically related to this. In that part of its work which determines the reality and nature of moral obligation from the constitution and action of the human mind, moral science joins with psychology in the investigation of man's mental capacities and powers. Ever since the days of Aristotle ethics has been seen to have real psychological basis and pre-suppositions. Yet, as a result of the later general subsuming of ethics under religious and theological precepts, this basis received but little distinct investigation till the time of Shaftesbury who, though failing to give adequate or correct account of it, brought it prominently forward. Mental science is essentially conditional for moral science. The behests of duty are provided for and sanctioned in human nature. The moral discriminations and convictions emerge as psychical phenomena. "To understand what man ought to do, it is necessary to know what he is." In the very structure and adjustment of his powers, it becomes apparent that he has been made for duty and organized under obligations.

But while psychology and ethics both study the powers and functions of the soul, they do so with different aims. The one has no aim beyond a knowledge of the phenomena and laws of the mind as mind. The other studies it with a view to the light which this knowledge sheds on the problems of virtue and duty. There are, indeed, some questions in ethics that transcend the province of psychology, and belong to the further realm of metaphysics— as, for instance, the validity and ground of the distinction between right and wrong—yet, so far as it is the science of conscience or of man's moral nature, it is thoroughly psychological. And well would it have been for moral science if, instead of speculatively and arbitrarily theorizing on the subject, it had more critically, fully, and exactly searched out the real facts in actual psychology and moved forward always toward the conclusions necessitated by these fundamental and abiding realities.

Relation to Natural Theology

(2) To Natural Theology. As Natural Theology seeks to determine the existence, character and will of God as Creator and Moral Governor of the world, and the consequent relations and responsibilities of men, it covers, to some extent, the same ground as a system of ethics constructed simply upon the basis of reason and the data found in man's nature and place. Both, if properly drawn out, bring to view the reality of "a power that makes for righteousness" in the natural constitution of the world, and exhibit the laws of obligation that bind men under the action of conscience. Both treat of the fact and authentications of human duty. A science of ethics, as well as a theology, may be constructed, apart from supernatural revelation, from the data of reason and nature alone. The possibility of this is implied in Rom. 2:14, 15. This would be a system of natural ethics. There is still, however, a large difference—though theology and ethics be kept apart from the teachings of special revelation. For Natural Theology keeps more prominently and controllingly in view the being and character of God, and aims more distinctly to produce the religious sentiments, while authenticating the reality and action of the moral law. Ethics, on the other hand, puts the facts of human nature and life into the front and includes the religious element only as a consequential, though necessary, inclusion.

Relation to Christian Theology

(3) To Christian Theology, or revealed religion. As this is the fullest disclosure of the duty of man, in all his relations, to God, to his fellow-men, and to his own end, it is not surprising that for so many centuries, the treatment of morals was made simply a part of general theology, and merely distinguished as Moral Theology. In the modern separation of ethics from theology and treatment of it as a science, it is not meant to deny the close affinity between the two investigations or the rich illumination

that duty receives from supernatural revelation, but only to trace out more distinctly and fully, in independent and scientific form, the deep and immovable foundations of the principles of duty in the very constitution of man and the world. This exhibition of the natural basis of ethical law and obligation becomes an independent and generic enforcement of the principles of righteousness. It gives a philosophic vindication of one of the first assumptions of Christianity—the supremacy of the law of rectitude for human life. And Christianity is vindicated and exalted when it comes recognizing and confirming all the principles and duties discoverable in our moral nature, and adding a supernatural disclosure of the way in which righteousness may be established in our lives, and men may attain their right character and destiny.

Christianity, while much more than this, appears as a divine re-publication of the ethical truth which from the first has been incorporated in the organization of humanity. In it the light of conscience is supplemented and made clear. The ethics of human reason and those of revelation thus cover, to a great extent, the same ground. When correctly read they are never in conflict, but in harmony. Both show man to be under moral law—and under broken law, that is, under sin. But the light of the Scriptures is broader and fuller. For in addition to their confirmation of a natural ethic for man, they disclose a scheme of redemption, with otherwise undiscoverable moral relations and obligations, introducing new and vital elements into the science of ethics. The inclusion of these elements and truths turns pagan or natural ethics into Christian.

Whatever interpretation may be given by different Christians to the redemption thus disclosed, the ethical teaching of the Sacred Scriptures, by universal consent, surpasses, in clearness, elevation and completeness, every other ethical view or system in the world. The loftiest philosophical thought has reached no higher summit—and has climbed to its best only in the light which Christianity has supplied. No system of morals is now worthy of the name that fails to avail itself of its ethical teaching. Only when this is properly included, illuminating natural ethics with its supernatural light, can we have the whole view of human duty. He who refuses the Christian grade and completeness of moral view goes back from the full daylight into the obscure dawn before the morning. Nevertheless the natural basis of ethical laws needs to be clearly apprehended and distinctly borne in mind. In these days when the foundations of all truths are put to scrutinizing tests, it is of fundamental importance that, through the verifying processes of careful science, we shall recognize the ethical verities and responsibilities, affirmed by revelation, as primarily and immutably a part of the very nature of man and the constitution of the world.

CHAPTER II

THE FACT OF MORAL DISTINCTIONS

Moral Distinction

The primary fact underlying the science of ethics is the great phenomenon of moral distinctions in the world. Scarcely anything in human life has been more conspicuous and indubitable than the existence of ideas of right and wrong and their application to human conduct. This has characterized mankind everywhere and in all ages. Its prevalence is as broad as humanity. A phenomenon so universal and permanent must necessarily be regarded as in some way organic in the human constitution. It calls for examination and justifies scientific inquiry into its cause and implications.

The certainty and largeness of the phenomenon become deeply impressive when it is traced out and fairly considered.

Revealed in Personal Consciousness

1. The distinction between right and wrong appears in every man's personal consciousness. Each one is directly and fully aware of it in his own case. He approves and condemns on this basis, and in doing so finds himself in harmony with a principle marking the sentiments of others around him. He passes quick, spontaneous judgments on his own conduct and on that of his fellow-men. The distinction, to greater or less degree, shapes itself into a sense of obligation and a law of duty. Nothing can wipe it out from his knowledge and feelings.

Incorporated in Social Organism

2. It is found incorporated into the social organism. What each man is conscious of doing in his own inner life, society, in its solidarity or constitutional unity, is found doing and enforcing. Organic humanity reveals the presence of the ethical conception and sure lines of its action everywhere. However diverse may be its judgments, there is such a thing as a public conscience that holds up conduct to favor or reprobation, not simply as beneficial or injurious but as being intrinsically right or wrong.

The social constitution is in fact framed together under the human capacity and necessity of perceiving and fulfilling the duties that arise in the inter-relations of associated life. For, the very laws and administrations on which the social order and welfare are dependent, and through which they are in a measure secured, are the embodiment of the ethical ideas and judgments of the people. No adjustment of relations is possible except upon this foundation. The obliteration of these ideas would mean social anarchy. "Society," says Prof. Borden P. Bowne, "in its organized form, is a moral institution with moral ends. However selfish individuals may be, they cannot live together without a social order which rests on moral ideas."

Witnessed in History

3. The great volume of history is witness to the universal phenomenon. Its records testify to the presence and action of the moral distinctions everywhere and in all the ages of the world. Whether these records present the customs and habits of early tribes, the rise and fall of nations, the reigns of princes and emperors, the exploits of generals and conquerors, the march and overthrow of armies, the relentless cruelty of tyrants or the noble service of patriots and benefactors, the establishment of just institutions or the miseries of the people where the oppressor's millstones grind on, all the pages are replete with evidence that men, around all the globe and through all the centuries, have been wont either to accuse or excuse the conduct and motives of

one another according to some standard of moral judgment or sentiments of right and wrong. It is true that from some pages of history the moral sense seems darkened out of sight. They bring before us thousands of men, often the most conspicuous in the ever-changing drama of public life, from whose thinking the notions of right and wrong seem to have been wanting or obliterated, acting only from selfishness, avarice, or ambition, monsters of injustice, heartlessness, cruelty and blood. Many of its chapters are but the sickening stories of tribal and national feuds and wars, of crime, plunder and devastation, of hate, scheming and treachery, of thirst for power, fame and treasure, of moving armies and fields of carnage and fire-swept lands, seeming to report that the moral sense had no place or force whatever in the men who were the actors in those scenes. But these chapters of lurid crime and wrong, like the records of crime today, do not represent all the thought of the humanity of such times. They tell of the men and deeds that most completely defied the moral ideas that belonged to their own nature, and whose remorseless wrong-doing evoked the deep, indignant reprobation of the thousands and millions of innocent and injured sufferers. And when the pen of history, with eye on the relations of cause and effect and the unfolding issues of such flagrant violation of right and justice, has traced the steps of a divine Nemesis, a stern Avenger, following the guilty, age after age, the record proves to be, all the more emphatically, a ceaseless testimony to the great fact of moral distinctions as a world-wide and ceaseless phenomenon of human life.

Shown in All Religions

4. The religions of the world all show the same fact. While these present a Godward side and express the perpetual human need of union and fellowship with the infinite divine Source of all Good, they at the same time testify to a distinctively moral constitution and action of human life. The sense of obligation, duty and guilt appears in the warp and woof of religion everywhere. While with a singular breach with reason religious rites and practices here and there have shown a wide departure

from correct moral principles, yet the religious consciousness of the race has been almost a synonym for the action of the moral sense. In all lands and all ages this consciousness has carried with it, in greater or less clearness and force, a conviction that the Power above men not themselves is a Power that makes for righteousness, establishing and enforcing principles of duty among men. And the various religions of mankind, especially those of monotheistic teaching and more distinct development, present clear and emphatic codes of moral principles and requirement. Some of them are resolvable largely into philosophies of life, with ethical directions for the regulation of conduct. In the Egyptian Book of the Dead, which belongs to the age of the pyramid builders, from 2000 to 3000 B. C., we find set forth a morality marked by surprising breadth and purity. In all the widespread religions of Asia, some of them emerging out of the darkness of prehistoric times, the Akkadian and Babylonian, Zoroastrianism, Brahmanism, Confucianism, Buddhism, Tâoism, Shintoism, and Mohammedanism, with their countless millions of followers, everywhere the constitution of man and social life is recognized as laid in laws of moral obligation and order, and religious life, in greater or less degree, is called to aspire to that which is judged to be right and good. Ancient Druidism was strongly marked by its emphatic moral tone. No Christian needs to be reminded with what sublime distinctness Christianity, with its redemption economy, declares the eternal distinction between moral good and evil, and calls men to peace and blessedness through faith and righteousness.

Religion, it is to be remembered, is in the broadest sense a fact of humanity. The distinguished anthropologist Quatrefages is sustained by the fullest evidence when he asserts that man is essentially a religious being. It appears in every tribe on earth. Moral conceptions and sentiments, however faint and faultily applied, are a part of this omnipresent religious mind of the race.

Pervades Literature

5. Such moral conceptions pervades the general literature of the world. Wherever a people has progressed in culture

sufficiently to create and preserve a literature, it is found to be a many-tongued witness to a recognized difference between right and wrong. In its pages these discriminations appear as a never-ceasing characteristic of human thought. They come to us out of the remotest past and from regions untaught by the Decalogue of Sinai. They illuminate, as already implied, the sacred books of India, China, Egypt, Persia and Babylonia, as well as the classic writings of ancient Greece and Rome and the Saga writing of Northern Europe. They not only form the body of the moral disquisitions of Socrates, Plato, Aristotle, Cato, Cicero, Seneca, Marcus Aurelius and many others, but color and shape the drama and lyric poetry in which the thought and sentiment of the race have been embalmed. To see illustrations of this we need only read the tragedies of Sophocles, for instance Œdipus Tyrannus, lines 863–871, or Antigone, lines 449–460, or listen to the verse of Horace, Book III, Ode 3, tracing the supremacy and triumph of a consciousness of right over all other authority and power. With the advance of humanity as the centuries have passed away literature is more and more the representation of human sentiment and life under the action and reaction of these ethical discriminations in the ever-changing conditions of the world. Philosophy and science and fiction and poetry and politics and jurisprudence are occupied in dealing with the principles and questions thus raised, and our modern libraries are largely the accumulated treasures of the thinking world on the significance and application of these principles.

Anthropological Confirmation

6. The ethnic and anthropological information of the present day reports no people or tribe, even the rudest, altogether without moral ideas and some measure of application of them to conduct. Enthusiastic scientists, travelers and missionaries, traversing the earth, have thoroughly established this point. Often, indeed, has the universality here asserted been disputed. Reports were brought of tribes discovered altogether destitute of the ethical sense. But closer inspection of the tribal and personal life has corrected the first impression, and evidences of the

disputed fact have become indubitable. A low and confused manifestation had been mistaken as none whatever. In degraded and besotted conditions of human life, it is altogether reasonable to believe that the particular discrimination in question would appear only in the crude and uncertain forms in keeping with the undeveloped grade of all the functions of thought and sentiment. The sunken humanity has carried down and buried its proper and normal manifestations almost out of sight. As soon as uplift comes to a tribe, the powers of moral discernment and knowledge, whose action was scarcely discoverable before, emerge in unmistakable certainty and force. And no phenomenon that science is seeking to investigate today can be more justly regarded as universally human than the fact under consideration.

Not Affected by Explanations

7. It needs to be distinctly fixed in mind that this great fact is not at all affected by any offered theory of its cause and significance. It stands independent of any particular explanation of it, and indeed of all solutions. If, for instance, the origin of these moral judgments should be traced back and accounted for, as is done by Herbert Spencer, as the result of accumulated experiences of utility, gradually organized and inherited as spontaneous approval and disapproval, the theory still recognizes the fact of ethical judgments while endeavoring to account for them. Or, when the older utilitarianism seeks to explain them as resolvable into the pleasure or satisfaction men feel toward certain forms of conduct or principles of behavior that are found to be useful and promotive of happiness, the fact still remains that judgments of right and wrong are actually established and dominate the thought and life of men. The very attempt to identify the virtues of life with its utilities, while making the virtues only its utilities, concedes that the obligation to them is part of the recognized reality of human life. Or, further, should a bolder and more radical view allege that these notions of right and wrong are mere matters of taste and prejudice, a fictitious product of adventitious circumstances and education, without verity or validity at bottom, the offered explanation would be

simply a denial, but no disproof of the fact concerned. For it would amount to a claim that in the absolute sense one thing is essentially as good as another, and would thus disregard the real affirmation as it stands in the moral judgment of mankind. Such a claim, it has been well said, no theorist of the present day would pretend to maintain outside of his closet. Not in any race or people has the ethical sense allowed that essentially and at bottom all acts are equally right. This is the very point of the great phenomenon presented. Whatever may be the final explanation of it, somehow or other the reason, sentiment and practical sense of mankind insists on a real difference, and look upon all denial of the distinction as a manifest and intolerable absurdity.

The universal recognition of this distinction, revealed in every man's consciousness, involved in the organic relations of society, testified to everywhere in the pages of history, embodied essentially in the religious nature and sentiments of mankind, woven into general literature, found today unmistakably in the thinking, laws and customs of all races and tribes, and acknowledged in the philosophical view of humanity wherever man is studied, irreducible as a fact by any account of its genesis or explanation of its significance, presents the occasion and primary materials of ethical science. The great phenomenon calls for investigation. We want to know the reasons for it and the import of it.

Theoretical Ethics

CHAPTER III

FACULTY OF MORAL DISTINCTIONS—THE EXISTENCE OF CONSCIENCE

The Moral Faculty

The great fact of moral distinctions, found to be universal in human thought and life, must be traced back to the particular power of the mind which discerns and feels these distinctions. Back of the phenomenon must be recognized the psychical capacity and action out of which the discriminations arise. The moral faculty answers to and in part accounts for the moral fact. In modern general literature it is usually called the conscience. Ethical science properly accepts the designation. It is sometimes called the moral consciousness, or the moral sense. It expresses a power of the personal *ego* or self to make the moral discrimination and discern the obligation to rectitude. Without such power, as an adequate capacity for the ideas, it is plain that the ethical judgments could not arise. The very idea of obligation, the ethical "ought," would be wanting. The whole realm of what this science considers would be a blank. In the moral faculty or conscience itself, as the immediate source of the ethical distinctions and laws of duty, we are furnished with additional material for this study.

No particular stress is here laid on the term "faculty," as a designation of the moral power. There is, indeed, no validity in the claim of some recent psychologists that the term must be abandoned on the ground that psychology discovers only mental acts, without a psychic subject with distinct faculties back of the

27

acts. Yet the term faculty has often been used and understood in a way inconsistent with the essential and conscious unity of the personal *ego* or self, making the soul seem a bundle of independent and separately acting parts of a psychical organism. The perfect oneness of the personal self must be maintained, and the term faculty, when used for any form of psychical ability, must be understood simply as expressing the soul's capacity or power to do any specific form of work, or to act in any particular and distinctively definable way, as, for instance, to know, to feel, to will, to remember, to compare. In this sense the use of the term stands fully justified in psychological usage and propriety. But the reason for abating from the claim of strict exactness in the term in this connection is that the conscience, in its full conception and action, as will hereafter appear, while exhibiting a specific and simple power as its central reality, will be found to include also subordinately the conjoint action of several other forms of psychical power. It stands for a complex of capacities and powers. This will appear when we reach its analysis. But the question of the absolute simplicity of the faculty does not affect the substance of our inquiry into its existence nor the propriety of employing the term for the power in its totality. For, as naming the central and decisive reality in the conscience, it is justly spoken of as a special faculty. Even when it is viewed as standing for a complex of powers converging, in their functions, to the discernment of moral distinctions and the reality of duty, it has sufficient individuality to be rightly and scientifically designated in this way. The question to be considered, and upon which the logical conclusions of the science will depend, is not its absolute simplicity, but the fact of such a power as a normal part in the soul's essential constitution of powers. If the power be found integral and normal in the soul's actual capacities, we have all that is essential for the foundation of ethics.

The existence of the conscience as a specific and natural faculty of discernment of right and duty may seem to the student or reader to need no formal proof, as something substantially everywhere acknowledged. But as various theories undertake to question its existence, in the sense thus explained, and resolve the affirmations of right and duty into pseudo-products developed in a roundabout way, or by some illusive transformation of ideas or sentiments given by the other faculties of the soul, ideas or sentiments which in fact are really unethical, it becomes necessary to vindicate the asserted existence of this moral faculty.

Moral Distinctions Prove Conscience

1. The primary and fundamental evidence is the great fact, already set forth, of the moral distinctions which arise out of its action and fill personal consciousness and the life of the world with their attesting presence. The known object implies a power by which it is known. Without the faculty, in the sense of a power to know, the knowledge here in question could not exist. Its existence is proof of the reality and action of the faculty perceptive of it. The only alternative to this would be a total denial of the ethical distinction, even as a genuine phenomenon, and an assertion that the supposed knowledge of it is, and always has been, illusory and unreal. And this would be equivalent to a claim that men may and should abandon the ethical distinction and believe that there is absolutely no moral difference between justice and injustice, between kindness and hatred, between truth and lying, between friendship and treachery, between charity and murder. And this again would mean that we are to repudiate, as without validity, the whole notion which the ages, especially the most intelligent and best ages, have cherished, that man is capable of character, as good or bad, excellent or blameworthy. But this whole alternative becomes impossible, by reason of the necessary and invincible contrary judgment by which the moral distinctions are affirmed as actual and valid for human life. The faculty of moral discernment proves its existence by making the contrary of its discernment an impossible conception.

The Moral Perceptions Peculiar

2. Its existence is further proved by the unique and peculiar character of its data or perceptions. These are unlike any other, *su ig eneris.* They are original and cannot be deduced from other data. The ethical percept is something that can be understood

only in terms of itself. It cannot be described or expressed in the terms of the percepts or knowledge given by the other faculties of the soul, either general or special, either separately or in combination. Hence we must, according to all sound psychological procedure, postulate a special faculty, as distinctive and normal as is the percept, for this original and irresolvable ethical idea.

A little explanation will help to show this. Let us make search for the ethical idea or perception among the well-known data of the other faculties. Manifestly it is not given by the "sense-perception," for it presents none of the physical properties which this makes known. Clearly, too, it is not created by the "consciousness," which presents simply the states or acts of the mind, with the personal self as their subject, but which does not itself originate the states or acts it reveals—any more than does the light of the morning create the objects of the landscape which it discloses. Further, it is evidently not given by the power of "representation," for this merely reproduces and re-knows what was before known through the "sense-perception" and revealed in "consciousness," revived in the form of memory or rearranged and recombined in the forms of the constructive imagination. It supplies no original data. It, further still, cannot be the product of the "logical" faculty, as the power or function of discursive reasoning, because this originates no new material, but only reconnects and judges of relations in the material already known, simply dealing with ideas furnished to it. Nor can the ethical percept, as an intuition to the obligation to rectitude, be at all identified with the *a priori* ideas of time and space, or the categories of substance and attribute, identity and difference, means and end, or the law of causation. And yet it stands out in an originality as positive and distinct as do any of the unquestionable data or percepts of the soul's acknowledged specific faculties.

Just as little can the ethical idea, as the discrimination of right and wrong, be referred to the "sensibility," as the pleasure or dislike with which we regard what is found useful and conducive to enjoyment or the reverse. For, though a certain pleasure is connected with the ethically right, this specific feeling follows, and is dependent on no other perception than of the right. It is a satisfaction which the ethically good thus awakens. But the knowledge which experience gives of what is useful and conducive to enjoyment is generically different from the moral idea and its sense of obligation. Utility and the ethical discrimination are not the same conception. They belong to two diverse realms of thought and knowledge. Whatever relations may be traced between them, they cannot be identified or held as convertible percepts. The autonomous imperative of the ethical idea often positively prohibits the very things men judge to be profitable and pleasurable. It is a remarkable fact that the testimonies from literature and life to the phenomenon of moral distinctions everywhere maintain the difference between the idea of right and that of the pleasurable or profitable. What is right is one thing; what is agreeable is another thing. The two conceptions are not identical, but are often placed in immediate and irreducible antithesis. Those who do right, choosing it and heroically loyal to it despite the appeals of ambition, the temptations of avarice, the enticements of ease, and the favor or the wrath of the wicked, are approved and honored. To such the gates of the divine favor and recompense are pictured as ever standing open.

There is another consideration in this connection which shows beyond question that this ethical faculty, whose action is everywhere traceable, is not to be confounded with mere intellectuality or the action of simply the general intellectual powers. It exhibits itself in a distinct line of working and results, like a particular current in the common sea, and often in open contrast. It is a peculiar and significant fact, often observed by historians, that as the civilizations of antiquity, of Assyria, Egypt, Phoenicia, Greece and Rome, advanced in intellect they declined in morals. Intellectualism may be at its height while the moral side of life may suffer a submergence beneath the floods of luxury and refined social vices. Buckle confesses that intellect and morals are not only distinguishable, but separable. Herbert Spencer says: "The belief in the moralizing effects of intellectual culture, flatly contradicted by facts, is absurd *a priori*." Lord Wolseley makes a statement not flattering to the boasted advantage claimed for simple intellectualism: "The virtue of the Zulu women was superior to that of any civilized people I know of." The function of the conscience in human nature and life stands clearly distinguishable from the common data and powers of mere intellectualism. The world will not be ethically saved by intellect alone. The conscience must dominate mere intellectual results and forces. And the high distinctive place and peculiar character of the conscience-perception is seen when it is thus observed that the perception is not of something that is, but of what ought to be, in the sphere of conduct and character. Its object is apprehended as lying in the ideal realm of obligation. The reality perceived is transcendent, as what should be in life, in order that life may accord with a super-sensible reality in the realm of righteousness. It as truly reaches beyond sense as do the intuitions of time and space or the law of causation; and, as truly as they, it calls for the recognition of a special and original psychical faculty or provision, among the powers of the soul, for its perception. The conscience,

"Deep-seated in our mystic frame,"

discerns a law of righteous obligation, which is not the dictate of mere desire or pleasure or self-advantage, but a law established at once over us and in us, not dependent on our will or choice but demanding conformity of will and choice to itself.

Feelings from Conscience Perceptions
3. The existence of the conscience as an integral power of the human constitution is evidenced also by the special feelings which attend its perceptions. They are distinctively peculiar. This is illustrated in the sense of obligation arising from the idea of right and the perception of duty. It is even more clearly illustrated in the satisfaction which attends and follows duty done, and the remorse which follows wrong or crime committed.

The sense of obligation, *i. e.* the emotion awakened by the perception of obligation, is unique among the emotions of the sensibility. In the presence of recognized right or wrong men feel bound to correspondent action as they feel bound under no other perceptions. The conscience, indeed, uses no compulsion, but it presents the right or wrong and correspondent obligation. Freedom is not annulled, but appealed to. The feeling, as the sensibility excited, is the feeling of ought or ought not, added to the perception of it. Nothing like this appears in connection with any of the other perceptions. We may perceive truth, but if the truth is not the particular truth of obligation itself, there is only the pleasure, gratification or admiration in its discovery and attainment. We may perceive beauty, but if the beauty be apart from that of ethical excellence, the feeling is simply aesthetic and different from the obligatory feeling: "I ought." We may perceive utility or understand what is simply profitable, but the feeling awakened is but desire. All these and like simply intellectual perceptions awaken no sense of obligation to cherish any special sentiments or perform any special acts. But as soon as men, in pure and normal state of their rational and emotional nature, perceive the right as over against the wrong, the sensibility which always in greater or less degree responds to every act of knowledge, presents a form of feeling, in the ethical "ought," generically different from the feelings that arise out of all other kinds of knowledge. This feeling is itself a part and parcel of the aggregate or complex of the conscience. But its presence marks the conscience as a special power normally constituent of human nature.

The other moral emotions named, viz.: satisfaction in duty done and remorse or compunction for wrong, bring us to the same conclusion. These feelings are *sui generis*. They are distinctively characteristic, and are never called forth but in connection with the moral intuitions. These peculiar satisfactions or compunctions never appear upon perception of a truth of mathematics or a fact in chemistry or a gem of art. Such knowledge evokes no sense of duty and is followed by no feeling of remorse or rush of compunction, flooding the soul with self-condemnation. A sense of loss, in failing to gain a possible advantage, is incapable of being confounded with the feeling of having done wrong. Some of the highest elevations of ethical satisfaction are felt when men have maintained their fidelity to the right in face of the most enormous losses and of the most desolating sufferings. The deepest remorse the human soul ever knows may spring up in view of ways and acts which have given men all the things they have coveted and judged to be the most useful and enjoyable. There must surely be a special power whose peculiar discernments call the sensibilities into such unique and peculiar forms of feeling.

Conflict of Moral Judgments

4. This conclusion is not weakened, as has sometimes been supposed, by the diversity and seeming conflict of moral judgments among men. This diversity seems, in the view of many persons, inconsistent with the supposition of a conscience, in the sense given. The fact of such diversity is freely conceded. The progress of history shows many changes in moral judgments. An advance is clearly traceable, in which once accepted rules of conduct have been superseded by different requirements. Things approved in one land and tribe are condemned in another. Pascal has said that conscience is one thing north of the Pyrenees and another south. In every community what some look upon as right others declare wrong. Infanticide, which under our civilization is punished as murder, on the banks of the Ganges has been esteemed a high religious duty. Polygamy, which our government is trying to wipe out as an immorality and foul blot, is held by the Mormons as a sacred right. Slavery is still regarded by some as right though condemned by the convictions of the nation as morally indefensible. Most startling diversities and contrasts are continually appearing. Hence it has often been said that our moral judgments rest, in fact, on no original and permanent principles discerned by a distinct and universal faculty of the soul, but are a purely adventitious and accidental product, shaped in ideas that come of circumstances, education or the shifting spirit of the age. The law of morality is reduced to the dictates of expediency or to sentiment and caprice born of our changeful desires. This virtually denies both the validity of the ethical behests and the reality of an ethical faculty provided for perception of rectitude and duty. But the difficulty from this diversity and apparent contradiction loses its force when

carefully considered. It disappears when we recall the following indubitable facts:

Ethical Sense Persists

First, that in the midst of this variety and conflict in the moral judgments, the ethical sense still persists in maintaining its function. If convicted of acting inconsistently, it still acts. Though it is found judging differently, it still judges, asserting its place and office, and imposing its decisions as obligatory in conduct. Under the view alleged in the objection, the sense of obligation ought to disappear, its supposed authority having been explained away. The person finds that in very truth the moral behest, though in him is not of him, is not of his will or choice, but arises out of the necessary action of a power that he cannot displace by refusal to obey it. The faculty or power does not consent, so to speak, to omit or withdraw its ethical distinction and assertion of duty. It does not abdicate, when men allege the illegitimacy of its authority.

Agreement in Judgments

Secondly, that while there is diversity as to many points, there is none in its judgments as to the great body of virtues and vices of human life. As to all the leading qualities of character and conduct there is full and universal agreement. With respect to all the cardinal virtues, such as justice, kindness, veracity, love, courage, fidelity, generosity, the moral judgments approve them as the magnet owns its pole, in all the multiform relations and offices of life. On the other hand, injustice, falsehood, enmity, treachery, cruelty, adultery, theft, murder and similar dispositions and acts in their thousand forms of unmistakable manifestation, are universally condemned. There is no question anywhere around our globe that one who deliberately kills his mother or mangles his father, or tortures the innocent or defrauds his friend, is a wrong-doer, of abhorrent guilt. Over almost the entire broad field of moral obligation there is a consentient, clear and consistent judgment by the moral sense of man in all ages and places. It is only along dividing lines, wider or narrower as they may be, that, by reason of the fainter presence of the moral element or the complexity of the relations concerned, the moral judgments exhibit this diversity or act with less assured and certain accuracy. The perplexity and difference find place only in limited degree and on remoter points, where the distinctions are so subtle as to require the nicest balancing of all the complex relations and elements which develop the ethical obligations.

If, indeed, the conscience reported entirely different codes throughout, from bottom to top and from center to circumference, or codes with contradictions as to the cardinal virtues and vices, then we might well question the existence and action of a real, original and normal faculty as actually perceiving a real moral distinction and principle of duty. But if such diversities are found only in limited degree, on marginal ground and in complex situations, we are simply in the presence of a fact of great similarity of the conscience with all the rest of the finite and fallible faculties of the human mind. Upon a hundred points of practical morals the intelligent conscience would be likely to agree quite as well as the judgments of men in any other sphere of practical knowledge and life.

Agreement in Principles

Thirdly, that even with respect to the cases in which there is the most startling diversity, there is often an underlying agreement, overlooked by superficial thought. Take, for instance, the Hindu mother's act of infanticide. Underneath her act and guiding it, is one or the other, or possibly both, of these principles: 1. Whatever sacrifice God calls for ought to be made; or, 2. Whatever is best for the child ought to be done. Falsely taught to believe that God calls for the sacrifice of her child, or that this surrender of it to him is the best thing for it, the mother makes the offering. Essentially as to the principles from which she acts her conscience and the Christian conscience are at one. But she has been misled as to the will of God. Her understanding is without correct information as to matters of fact, and she applies mistakenly the principles of duty which are in her moral nature. Take, again, the crimes of religious intolerance and persecution. The religious zealot believes that every man is to be, without weakness or shadow of turning, faithful to the truth. So also does the dissenter from the creed which the persecutor defends. They agree as to the underlying principle of action. Each feels bound by the same ethical law of "fidelity to the truth," but the persecutor is in grievous error in understanding that this fidelity binds him to coerce the mind of his dissenting brother.

Difference of Perceptions

Fourthly, the difference must be clearly kept in view between the essential ethical perception, viz.: the distinction of right and wrong with the involved obligation, and the application of that perception—between the primary and secondary moral judgment. The primary is the intuition of the law of right, the secondary affirms the quality of right or wrong with respect to particular actions. In the one case the moral sense perceives that justice, love, veracity, kindness, etc., are right, and injustice, hatred, falsehood and cruelty are wrong; in the other the judgment is concerned with the further question whether this, that, or the other act comes under one or the other of these categories. The fundamental ethical distinction and obligation, with approval of justice, truth, etc., are generic, and altogether irrespective of any particular actions or instances. The secondary judgments apply the distinction to particular modes of conduct or forms of temper and feeling. The latter are only in part moral judgments, *i. e.* only so far as the particular feeling or deed exhibits to the conscience the presence of the ethical quality. It is an unquestionable fact that in many of the activities of life there are open alternatives of choice where the question of moral quality is not raised at all. As, for instance, between taking one path or another to a certain point, or in writing a letter with a pen or typewriter, the choice is morally indifferent. The decision involves no ethical judgment. But in most contemplated action there are relations that raise the question of right or wrong—in some cases only by remote implication, in others in clear and burning emphasis. There are degrees in this respect, all the way from the faintest glimmering of ethical quality to the boldest and most transparent certainty. We are by no means entitled to doubt the existence of conscience, because in all these unequal conditions, with imperfect knowledge of the relations of particular actions and feelings, it fails to apply its unchanging affirmations of generic duty, with equal or unmistaken certainty and exactness, to all the varied motives, feelings and deeds of men. It is clear how differing moral judgments may occur, without any impeachment whatever of either the ethical reality or the existence of the faculty for its discernment.

Infallibility Not Involved

Fifthly, we must add that the reality of this faculty, as an essential endowment of the human soul, by no means involves infallibility in its action. No one of the human faculties is, in all its range and the application of its data, absolutely infallible, incapable of error or of being misled. The sense-perceptions, the memory, the logical power, the power of applying the notions of time and space, are all liable to error. Yet these are all original, constitutional and normal faculties of man, divinely-given guides for his self-direction and suited to the ends for which they exist. The reality of a faculty is not disproved by its fallibility. Finiteness, limitation and consequent incompetence to exclude mistake or only partial discernment, are no reason for denying the existence of any faculty within the range of its given action and real discriminations. The very errors that appear in its action are at once evidence of its existence and proof of limitations which harmonize it with the aggregate human psychology. The objection against the conscience from its fallibility, which is but another name for this diversity in its applicatory judgments, if applied to all the psychical faculties, would discredit the reality of the aggregate complex of the psychical powers and overthrow the basis of all our knowledge, even of that which is employed to effect such overthrow. No diversity occurs in the primary judgment of distinction between moral good and evil. As already explained, it is easy to see how differences varied and great, should appear in the application of the distinction to the complicated, obscure and ever-changing aspects and relations of human conduct.

Proofs Independent of Origin

5. These proofs of conscience as a distinct endowment of the human mind are independent of the whole question of the mode of its origin. For they consist of facts, as clear, peculiar, indisputable and irreducible as are the facts that guarantee any particular science whatever. They are capable of verification under perpetual tests, as they have been verified in the consentient experience of mankind in all its normally developed conditions. And the logic of the facts is altogether irrespective of any theory of the mode of the origin of conscience. It is needful that this point should be clearly fixed in mind, especially in view of the wide favor at present shown to the hypothesis of an evolutionary genesis of man. Except in the materialistic and atheistic form of the hypothesis the theory distinctly presents evolution not as the cause, but only as the mode of the creation of man with all his now given endowments. It is, of course, incumbent on the supporters of the hypothesis, in any form whatever, in order to vindicate its scientific claims, to show its competency to account for the existence and action of the moral faculty with its ethical discernment and law. An hypothesis that fails to solve any of the involved phenomena discredits itself, not the facts. So far as the materialistic, non-teleological form of evolutionism is concerned, which proposes matter and force as the full cause and account of man, it is condemned by its own utter inadequacy to explain the genesis of conscience with its moral law, as well as of the other great psychical realities in the nature and life of man. It is helpless before the task. Its only resource is to seek to resolve both the ethical fact and the ethical faculty into illusion. With respect to theistic evolutionism, which stands simply as an hypothesis of the mode of creation by God, the existence of the moral faculty may still be admitted, as having its all-suffient cause in the divine creative power as the source of all things. If, instead of an immediate creation of man, the idea of his gradual creation from the inferior animal orders be

maintained as the actual method of the divine work, then the law of evolution must be regarded as having been adjusted and used for the production of man with the faculty of moral discernment. The teleological principle, everywhere illuminating the structure of organisms and the constitution of life, must, from the first, have guided the development for this enthronement of right in the human personality. Asserting its method of a progressive genesis of conscience, this kind of evolutionism confesses its existence. Whether or not its account is satisfactory is another question, to be decided according to the evidence furnished. It is more than doubtful if it has yet succeeded in making clear the possibility of its origin under the hypothesis. Some serious difficulties have still to be overcome. If it ever does succeed it must be, not by denial of the conscience, but by showing the evolutionary movement in some way or other competent to its creation.

This lengthened presentation of the evidence of the existence of the conscience as an essential endowment and part of human nature, may seem to the reader to have been unnecessary or beyond the importance of the question involved. But, as will appear hereafter, the firm establishment of this point is vitally needful, in order to exclude various forms of erroneous teaching and secure a firm and immovable foundation for a just ethical system.

CHAPTER IV

THE FACULTY OF MORAL DISTINCTIONS—THE NATURE OF CONSCIENCE

In close connection with the indubitable fact of conscience, as an essential faculty of the human soul, follows a more careful inquiry into the nature of this faculty. It is necessary to ascertain precisely, if possible, what it is as a peculiar psychical power, as revealed and defined in and by its own action.

Right View Necessary

1. The importance of determining, at this place, the exact nature of the conscience is apparent from two considerations.

Scientific Accuracy

(1) Scientific accuracy in the whole ethical view is possible only through a true and thoroughly accurate understanding of the power that gives rise to the whole phenomenon of obligation. The final theoretical view is dependent on finding the truth at this point. Mistake or inexactness here must inevitably introduce, or at least allow, confusion or error in all the dependent questions of the science. A false conception of the conscience will at once mislead. Even an only partial or obscure view of it will fail to afford sufficient light for the subsequent steps of the investigation. A conception of it, with true and false elements combined, must necessarily introduce perplexity or contradiction and weaken or distort the conclusion.

41

Such differing views have in fact introduced the utmost confusion into the problems of this science. The conscience has sometimes been spoken of as an "instinct," which identifies it with the non-intelligent, blind action in the bee which builds cells after geometrical principles, or in birds or fishes which migrate with the changing seasons. Often it has been represented as but a special "feeling" or "sentiment" that arises inexplicably, if not fortuitously, prior to perception of any ethical quality, itself the basis of judgments of duty. Again it has been made to stand simply for accumulated or established approbative judgments from experiences of pleasure or advantage, transformed and fixed as rules of conduct. Sometimes it has been regarded as an immediate, almost supernatural "voice of God" within men, with its inexplicable direct imperative of duty. It is plain that these and other differing notions of conscience must always affect, as they always have affected, the whole theory of ethics.

Condition of Authority

(2) A right view of its nature is necessary to a correct conception of its authority. This makes the question more than simply speculative or important for correct ethical theory. It involves the interests of practical morality. The right of the conscience to rule us is sustained or denied according as one or another conception of its nature is entertained.

It is natural that we should feel prompted to examine the nature of a part of our constitution that is constantly obtruding its distinctions and asserting a ruling authority over us. As it has its place within us irrespective of our will and presents laws of duty to the will, we want to see on what ground its asserted authority can be justified. But not all views of its nature afford equal explanation of this peculiarity in its action. For instance, if the conscience be nothing but a blind, irrational "instinct," or a "feeling" without any perception of reality to give rise or right to the feeling, or if it be but a standard judgment of prudence or utility from experiences of what has been helpful or hurtful, perhaps slowly accumulated and hereditarily transmitted, a clear and rational ground of ethical authority cannot be made out. Such a power may indicate what is useful, but can, if this be all, impose on us no obligation. It may tell us what is pleasurable or desirable, but cannot speak to us concerning the other question: What is right? It cannot hold us guilty because we may choose to forego personal advantage or enjoyment. If, however, examination can show that the conscience is a faculty of actual perception, discerning a fundamental distinction between right and wrong and an immutable obligation to apply it in the constituted relations of life, its rightful authority is at once vindicated. It is seen to be an authoritative guide in its sphere of perception, as are the other cognitive powers, each in its own sphere of real knowledge. When it becomes clear that the moral faculty, in the presence of the existing conditions and relations of life, perceives what ought to be done, and what men are obligated to do, and what they cannot disregard without demerit, ill-desert or guilt, then the right of conscience to direct conduct is justified.

At any rate, whether the examination may confirm or discredit this claim of rightful rulership, the inquiry into the nature of the conscience is essential to a correct settlement of the great question of its authority and the grounds of it.

Question of Psychology

2. The primary and proper source of information to settle the question of the nature of this faculty is to be found, not in speculative theorizing or arbitrary assumptions, but in the actual working of the human mind. It is a psychological question, and must be settled, as all psychological questions must, by the facts as they are discovered in experience and consciousness. The method of inductive inquiry is here the true and essential one. The full phenomena of action must be carefully examined, analyzed and traced to their psychical genesis. Such examination can leave but little doubt in the conclusion. In the facts of consciousness, as found in connection with the operations of our minds in the sphere of moral self-determination and action, the entire movement can be observed, marked and recorded.

Place of Conscience

3. In a preliminary way, it must be noted and remembered that the power and action of conscience can have place only in connection with the total complex of man's psychical powers. It is not an isolated, independent faculty in the midst of the different powers of the soul. This truth will require fuller consideration in another place, but it is necessary to note it here so far as to show the essential psychological conditions of conscience.

The very possibility of such a faculty or power is conditioned in all the human faculties of intelligence, sensibility and choice, in which man becomes a moral agent. While the soul or self is a unit, its powers act under a law of inter-dependence, exhibiting a striking and beautiful order of conditioning and being conditioned, from the primary and fundamental forms of activity to those that are highest and crown all the rest. At the very base and beginning of its action are sense-perception and consciousness—these furnishing knowledge of the outer and inner worlds, of the realities and relations in the system of things in the midst of which man finds himself. Dependent upon the percepts by the senses and the states of consciousness thus furnished comes the further capacity of "representative knowledge" in the forms of memory and the imagination. Only as the original acts of perception and consciousness have supplied their data, is the memory or the imagination possible. But the representative power and action are then necessary to the action of the higher powers. Without memory the logical power, the discursive function in comparison, judgment and conclusion, in analysis, synthesis and systemization, would have no materials and could do no work. The mind could not do this advance work except upon the basis of work of a different kind done before. And then, too, the reason, as the power of intuitive or *a priori* truths, would be without a knowledge of the phenomenal world, in the midst of which, or on occasion of the experiences of which, these *a priori* truths appear and are seen to be necessary. The various kinds of knowing exercised by the undivided and indivisible self are plainly arranged in an ascending order, till at their summit they are crowned with the intuitional power which we may term, as we here do, the reason—the power of discerning necessary universal truths. But it is equally clear that of the powers below the reason—sense-perception and consciousness furnishing facts objective and subjective, memory restoring them before the mental eye, and the logical power rushing to necessary conclusions—none, either singly or together, can stand for the conscience. Sense and consciousness can give us only what is, not what ethically ought to be. The memory can but renew to mental view what was before known. The sense of logical necessity is clearly different from the perception of moral rightness and obligation. But the action of these antecedent powers or faculties supplies the conditions for the existence and action of the conscience—gives knowledge of the personal self and the relations of life, in the midst of which moral right and wrong and obligation and duty are developed and are seen to arise. Upon this knowledge, in which man knows himself and his relations to the world of which he forms a part, the soul rises to an outlook in the clear atmosphere of which the reality of ethical distinctions, duty and responsibility become visible. And to the crowning power of the reason, as rational insight, must be assigned the central function of this ethical perception of right and obligation—somewhat as to it belong, in another field of view, also the intuitions into the realities of time and space and the categories of substance, attribute, and causality.

This position of the conscience as, in its fundamental action, a form of rational intuition, among the summit forms of the mind's powers, makes evident its relation of dependence on the entire complex of psychical faculties which furnish the conditions for its discernments and imperative. But there is something more. As we shall yet see, its total function, in guiding the moral life, includes the action of many of the common functions of both intellect and sensibility.

4. The specific psychology of the conscience itself, under close and complete analysis, will disclose the following clearly distinguishable elements in its action. They reveal the nature of the conscience-power in its total complex reality. These elements

are not separable in fact, but are distinguishable in the analytic thinking that examines them.

Ethical Distinctions

(1) The primary element is a simple irreducible perception of the distinction between right and wrong. This is the first and fundamental ethical idea. In it we have the initial point in the moral action of the mind. "The universal ethical fact is the recognition of a distinction between right and wrong in conduct." This distinction appears among the necessary ideas of the human mind. It is a phenomenon in the psychology of the race. It is developed, in the presence of the facts and relations of life, as something provided for in the normal and necessary action of the rational self-conscious *ego*. It must be viewed as an "intuition" of the reason. It can not otherwise be accounted for. In its nature it is not a feeling, though it gives rise to feeling. It is not a volition, for it comes irrespective of choice and asserts its own rights before the will. It is not a mere experience, though it arises on occasion of experience. The idea stands for something beyond experience—experience being limited to the profitable, the enjoyable or the painful. We experience the useful and the agreeable, but the right, the ethical idea, must be perceived or rationally seen, as a supersensible reality in the ideal realm of the demands of duty. It is not a perception of relations themselves, but of a distinction as to something due in human relations and life.

If we describe this primary and fundamental distinction, as it appears in the action of the conscience, it will be found marked by the following characteristics. First, the distinction is perceived—a datum of the cognitive intellect. As discerned by the knowing faculty, its object, viz.: the distinction, exists. For knowing always involves that the thing known is. The distinction between right and wrong is real in the sphere of moral relations. Second, it is universal, marking the human mind's action everywhere and in all ages. Third, it cannot be obliterated. Through all questions about it and objections to its validity, it remains undestroyed and seemingly indestructible. It disappears only with the wreck of rationality itself. Fourth, it is unique and simple, an original perception, incapable of being resolved into more elementary ideas or deduced from them. Fifth, it is the first of its kind of discernments, *i. e.* of ethical perceptions.

Obligation Perceived

(2) Along with, though dependent on, the perception of the moral distinction between right and wrong, there is also a perception of obligation with respect to right and wrong—to do or not to do. This is an essential part of the aggregate conscience-discernment. The perception of the right is thus the discovery also of law for conduct.

The soul, it must be specially noted, perceives this obligation as truly as it does the ethical distinction itself. The term "obligation" may express also a feeling, but the *ego*, or personal self, perceives the obligation before it feels it. For in all cases rational emotion or feeling can arise in the mind only as the mind discerns something to awaken it.

Belongs to the Agent

It is to be particularly observed, further, that the obligation, thus perceived and then felt, is perceived and felt as due by the moral agent with respect to right and wrong. The ethical quality of rightness belongs to the act or principle of action. The motive, the intention, the conduct of men, is in itself morally right or wrong, good or evil. But the obligation appears as what is owed by the moral agent to what is right. The relation between right and obligation corresponds to that between right and duty. Right is in the conduct; duty is for the responsible person. The terms express two sides in the ethical reality, the first the objective side, the second the subjective. The two imply and call for each other. The right in the contemplated action means obligation or duty in the person. To the right there is always a corresponding duty; for duty in fact expresses what is due to the right forever by all persons.

This perception of obligation, with its attendant feeling of it, is the central reality of the conscience. It is the very core of it. For in this the moral faculty carries and asserts its "imperative" for the regulation of conduct. On the basis of the idea of right, it affirms duty, and brings mankind under the reality and behests of moral law. The distinction of right and wrong, if conceived of as unattended with this further discernment of obligation, would manifestly fall short of establishing the principle of duty or fixing in the soul a conscious bond to righteousness. But in this further discernment is revealed the nexus that binds together perceived right and man's responsibility to it. Hence, this is the cardinal thing in the conscience, for which the ethical idea prepares, and upon which the moral life rests. It is the point at which humanity is organized under a moral constitution and the behests of moral law. It is the sublime endowment in which man's nature is capacitated for its position, as standing face to face with the sublimer reality of the divine government over the world.

It is to be distinctly observed, however, that the "imperative" disclosed in this perceived obligation, does not mean compulsion. The idea of "obligation" can have no place where there can be no choice as to accepting it. The whole sphere of morals, as we have already seen and shall need often to be reminded, exists, and can exist only in connection with personality or intelligent free agency. Its realm is that of freedom. Law in ethics is something in clear contrast with law in the processes of physical nature. The perception of it is not the perception of what must be or will be, or shall be, but what ought to be. Its appeal is to our freedom, and the duty is ideated before it is performed.

Further, it is well to observe here again how distinctly peculiar is this percept of obligation among the data of our cognitive faculties. The sense-perception notifies us of what is. So does the consciousness. Memory renews to consciousness a knowledge of what was. The logical processes reveal abstract relations. That two and two make four, or that a straight line is the shortest between two points, or that oxygen and hydrogen united in certain proportions form water, are truths distinctly known when the mind is directed to these subjects; but the perception of these truths is without the unique idea of obligation or the duty of cherishing any particular feeling or of conforming to a standard of righteousness. Only through the discernments of right and wrong by the conscience, is there given this peculiar intuition of the reality of obligation.

Moral Quality Identified

(3) A third thing to be marked in this psychological analysis of the action of conscience, and revealing its nature, is the affirmation of right or wrong to particular acts or principles of conduct. In this the function of conscience passes from its fundamental idea into the form of an applicatory judgment. The ideas of right and obligation are applied to the actual affairs and activities of life. The quality of right or wrong is connected with particular actions, feelings or purposes, and these are affirmed to be right or wrong according as they have or have not such moral quality. This application is both a perception and a judgment—a perception in that it sees the ethical quality in the deed or motive, and a judgment in that it affirms the connection. These judgments take the forms of approval or disapproval, as the conduct is discerned to be morally good or bad. It is plain that such judgments of application would be impossible were there not in the mind the fundamental ethical distinctions already explained.

Manifestly these judgments of application belong to the general judging power of the mind. All knowing may be said to be judging, or at least tends to take the form of judgment. They are specific here, only with respect to the material they take account of. They are the acts of the judging faculty in the sphere of applying the ethical distinctions and obligations. As a basis for the judgments, not only must the ethical distinction exist in the mind, but the action or conduct to be judged must be seen or understood in all its essential relations and motives. As duties are developed by relations, the moral character of the contemplated conduct or deed cannot be determined apart from a correct knowledge of those relations. The judging capacity will err without the light of true and full information concerning the place and purposes of the action. And its insights and affirmations will vary in their approximation to entire correctness according to the degree in which all the elements entering into the particular conduct are understood and considered.

Merit and Demerit Perceived

(4) The action of the conscience includes also perception of merit and demerit in connection with conduct. The meaning of these terms needs to be carefully defined and limited. They express something more than the simple approval or disapproval already noted in connection with the discernment of the rightness or wrongness of an action. The terms stand for a step of discernment and judgment beyond these, and denote the ethical reality of good-desert or ill-desert for the moral agent who conforms to rightness, or offends against its claims. He who conforms deserves well; he that offends deserves ill. They, therefore, mark distinctly and definitely the point in the psychology of the conscience where the faculty discerns that those who do right ought to receive favor and those who do wrong ought to experience disfavor. They express a principle of just consequences. The principle is, that for right conduct good is due, for wrong done evil is due. The wrong-doer is guilty, *i. e.* justly subject to punitive action. His deed deserves it for him. On the other hand doing right is worthy of reward, or of the good that befits the good done. The conscience discerns and affirms this reality of good and evil-desert.

Here is reached the psychological source of the great fact of responsibility in the world. It emerges into consciousness and into actual force in human life from this point in the disclosures and affirmations of the moral sense. Hence arises the unspeakably varied but ever persistent human necessity under which men are compelled to regard themselves and others as justly amenable to the law of moral consequences. Its application is seen in every sphere of life, personal, domestic, social, and national. A moral administration is seen in the world only as the administration is found to be conformed to and carrying out the principle of distributing good according to moral desert. Any failure in the adjustment of recompense or given good under this idea is felt to be a lapse from justice and proper order. It stands as something abnormal and monstrous. So firmly does the decision of conscience establish this principle of happy consequences as due to right conduct and punitive effects to wrong-doing, so strongly does it fix the conviction that the divine administration must on the whole adjust award and happiness on this basis, that thoughtful philosophers have ever been wont to find here one of the most assuring guarantees of a future life in which the fragmentary justice of this world will be filled out in fully given recompense.

It must be noted, as is apparent, that this merit or demerit does not belong to men's acts, but to themselves as the moral agents. To action and conduct pertain the moral qualities of rightness and wrongness, but what is done is itself altogether impersonal and not responsible for its own occurrence. The doer of the deed deserves whatever good or evil is due in connection with it.

The practical application of this principle of moral desert is found to be almost infinitely varied, both with respect to the import of the principle and the measure of merit and demerit. With respect to its *import*, good desert may mean simply that he who chooses the morally right is entitled to his own self-approbation and the approval of others and the moral excellence which he thus prefers. Or it may signify various degrees and kinds of more positive reward which the divine constitution and moral administration of the world may be adjusted to give in the way of happiness and the best external conditions of existence. On the other hand, the demerit of the wrong-doer may mean anything he deserves, from the simple loss of the moral good which he does not choose, to the extremest penalties, objective and subjective, which a righteous divine government may have to employ for the repression of wickedness. In its import, both merit and demerit may refer to endlessly varied experiences and forms of good and evil. With respect to the *measure* of merit and demerit and the adjustment of due recompense, a similar wide range of difference must be recognized when we come to the application of the principle to human acts and conduct. Conformity to right and offense against it are exhibited in myriad degrees under conditions as varied as are the positions and relations and inner state of all the individuals of the race. The very nature of different persons is in unequal adjustment to virtue and vice. Environment, too, brings stronger temptations to some than to others. Hereditary forces and early training strengthen or weaken the moral perceptions and forces. Thousands of differences perplex the attempt to equate the measure of moral desert to men. It can be determined only in full and perfect view of all the conditions within and the relations surrounding the moral agent; and the apportionment of the due award, it would seem, can be perfectly made only by a being of infinite knowledge and justice.

The measurement of merit and demerit is, however, but another form of judgments of application, in which the moral sense can act in only approximate determinations. Here variation and uncertainty find place. But there can be none as to the fact of good desert and guilt where right and wrong are done.

Emotions Awakened

(5) Emotions or feelings, awakened by the perceptions of right and wrong, obligation, merit and demerit, complete the action of conscience. These feelings are peculiar and original, unlike the feelings springing from any other perceptions and incapable of being resolved into or deduced from others. Psychologically, it is to be remembered, feeling is in no case a part of perception or cognition, but an additional psychical action of a different kind. "A purely cognitive intelligence might have perfect knowledge of things and their relations to itself; it might know that things, or courses of action, would destroy its own existence; it might even know that its own existence was about to be destroyed; but this knowledge alone would imply no feeling. Such intellect would be like a mirror; it would accurately reflect all that passed before it; but it would be as indifferent as the mirror." But knowing is followed by feeling, a different kind of action of the soul. This is not its action in the form of intellect, but in the form of sensibility. It is action of another order—not itself a cognition, but arising out of cognition. This is the place and relation of these

moral feelings. They are awakened in the soul by and through the ethical perceptions. They are determined by these, and form the final element in the total action of the conscience.

These moral feelings, while they form one class, as having their origin in the ethical discriminations, exhibit distinguishing differences. These differences develop in a twofold way, presenting special forms of feeling. They must be noted as they differ by these two conditions of their development.

Correspondent to Right or Wrong

First, according as the moral quality, the perception of which awakens them, is good or evil. The soul cannot discern the great distinctions between right and wrong without correspondent emotional awakening. The sensibility is moved by the perception, and takes the form of a feeling of approval for the morally good, and a feeling of reprobation for the wrong. Our language furnishes no single term to designate either of these feelings, but this phraseology is sufficiently descriptive to point them out. The feeling toward the right may be denoted as moral love; that toward wrong as moral aversion. When the quality of rightness or wrongness is exhibited in specially intense degree in particular conduct, the feelings may take the form of ethical admiration or of abhorrence.

Before and After Action

Secondly, as arising before or after the moral action. If the feeling is awakened in view of action proposed to be done, it may be described, in the absence of a more specific designation, as a sense of obligation to do or not to do the deed—this feeling of obligation being based on a perception of the obligation. From the intellectual discernment the emotional sensibility springs as a sentiment which forms part of the impelling force of conscience. When the feeling arises with respect to an act already done, it takes the nature of ethical satisfaction, a peculiar pleasure in which are blended a sense of self-approbation and of joy, if the deed be right; of self-reproach and remorse, if wrong. Remorse—

"a gnawing sense of guilt," whether the feeling be the slightest disquiet of emotion or of agonizing and unsolaceable compunction—appears to be the aptest term to express this state of mind.

Differences of Degree

Besides the differences thus arising, there are differences in the degree or intensity of these moral feelings. Innumerable causes may affect the differences in this respect. Personal temperament, acquired character, or external conditions may make the feeling greater or less. The mental organization of some persons is more emotional. Education may have given a peculiar development. Temporary circumstances may heighten the excitation. But other things being equal the degree of positiveness in the moral emotions is generally dependent on two things: (*a*) the clearness with which the moral distinction and the consequent obligation is discerned, and (*b*) the pureness and tenderness of the person's moral nature. If the ethical idea and obligation are unclearly seen or hardly seen at all, the impression in the feelings must be comparatively slight. But if seen under strong light and with their supreme import, the intuition impresses with greater force. So, too, the state of the whole moral nature is a reason of higher or lower moral sensibility. The more unblighted is the condition of personal life, the more is it responsive to the ethical discernment. Habitual refusal of duty, easy and indifferent familiarity with wrong-doing, or any continued enslavement of the higher nature to the lower, necessarily blunts the delicateness of the sensibilities and lowers the strength of the moral feelings. The process of injury may go on until a condition of callousness is reached which fulfils the striking description: "Seared as with a hot iron."

Motive Power

It is through these feelings that the conscience becomes a motive power for moral life. The perception of duty alone, as purely intellectual, would be, as said, "like a mirror accurately reflecting the ethical reality passing before it, but as indifferent as the mirror." But upon the perception the emotional nature springs into action. Knowledge, if at all, always goes into effect mediately through the sensibilities in which the soul is stirred by affections and desires. These may be toward moral good as truly as toward sensuous good. We may love the true and the beautiful and the right. We may love the right as right. According to our choices we make the ethically good our own and mold our life into its excellence and blessedness, or the contrary. These feelings are motive powers, bringing occasions for choices.

It is proper to take note, however, that it is only the feelings in view of the right or wrong of an act yet to be done, that are directly moral motives. For it is only through these that we are face to face with the question of choosing or refusing the right in the proposed conduct. The feelings that arise, as satisfaction or remorse after wrong acts, have no existence till the conduct is in retrospect, and can have no motive force for it. And when memory brings these experiences as motives for subsequent conduct, they stand mainly, if not wholly, as considerations for enjoyment. They are not feelings of pure obligation to rightness, but remembrances of pleasure or pain influential as prompting or dissuading on the lower ground of comfort. There is a generic and indelible difference between the feeling of duty, under the pure behests of right, and the natural desire to gain the enjoyment or avoid the misery which we have learned to anticipate from experiences in conduct. In the one case it presents love of the right as right; in the other a love of the more agreeable consequences of right. Unquestionably, indeed, a desire of the better consequences is a proper motive for choices. In these consequences virtue is proving its adaptation to bring its own reward. But the merit of virtue is not in seeking the reward, but in seeking virtue itself. The mercenary spirit is not the love of righteousness, nor as high as it.

5. This analysis makes clear the following characteristics of the conscience.

Conscience is Intellectual

First, it is primarily and fundamentally intellectual. It is a power of rational perception. It perceives, in direct or intuitive way, the primary ethical distinction between right and wrong, perceives the quality of rightness or wrongness in particular acts or conduct, perceives the obligation of the moral agent with respect to right and wrong, as also the merit or demerit of the moral agent. But along with and blended in inseparable concurrence, moves the function of the sensibility, in feelings of approval and obligation, satisfaction or remorse. Both the intellectual and emotional action of the soul are, therefore, included in what is named the conscience—the perceptive action, here as everywhere else, being primary and conditional for the emotional. If there were no ethical distinction perceived, none would be felt. The conscience, taken in its totality, thus includes both sides of the human psychology, the intellect and the sensibility, and it addresses its behests of duty to the will in its own peculiar way of moral law for conduct.

The strife between intuitional theories and sentimental theories of conscience is, therefore, composed by the concurrence of both knowing and feeling in the action of this power. But the intellectual part is necessarily logically prior to the emotional, and conditional for it. To make a feeling of obligation the basal fact in the psychology of conscience would be an inversion of the whole order of dependence revealed in consciousness. And, surely, the feelings here developed are rational, not physiological sensations. They cannot, for a moment, be identified with the physical sensations which condition the sense-perceptions. Their true place is among the rational emotions.

Sole Percept Moral Quality

Secondly, the sole object of perception by the conscience is moral quality—the quality of rightness or wrongness, together with the correspondent obligation. It is something supersensible and ideal; not actions themselves as known by sense, but their quality as morally good or evil as discovered by the ethical reason. The thing discerned by the conscience is generically different from the things discerned by the sense-perception or consciousness. Through our senses we know the whole world of objective existences, events and their relations; through consciousness the states, acts and experiences of the subjective personal self are given. But the conscience does not furnish us with a knowledge of any of the substances, events or relations which constitute the world about us or the world within us, but solely of the moral quality of conduct and sentiment, as duty is developed in these relations. It takes notice of the ethical character of the actions and motives of intelligent and responsible beings.

Conscience Acts of Necessity

Thirdly, the action of the conscience is marked by necessity. And by this we are to understand something more than the simple uniformity in which all the psychical activity, except that of the choices of the will, is held under "fixed laws of thought and feeling." The necessity here affirmed is that unique necessity which distinguishes and marks intuitive or *a priori* cognition, as of time, space, and causality. "Necessity" is justly conceded to be one of the criteria of these and other intuitional "first truths." It is not at the option of the human mind whether it will think the world under the relations of time and space, or events as occurring under the principle of causation. These are "forms of knowledge," knowledge of supersensible realities, that come not at our choice but by an unavoidable insight. The primary and fundamental ethical distinction belongs to such rational intuition, and is marked by the peculiar necessity of intuitional action. As on occasion of knowing material bodies with three dimensions, or of changes in consciousness or in the outer world, with the fact of co-existence or succession and duration, the phenomenal sphere is necessarily transcended and time and space are necessarily discerned, so when we understand the manifold relations in which our lives are to be lived, in which we may use our personal powers, either in harmony with or in violation of our given adaptations, and with either great injury or rich good to others, in the same necessary way the conscience must discern the distinction of right and wrong and the reality of duty.

The great implication in this necessity, as we shall hereafter see in examining the nature of virtue, is that the principle of righteousness or the law of duty is something that belongs to the objective order of the world as constituted by God, a divine reality permanent and immutable, not produced but perceived by the conscience. It is not made by man but finds him—finds him through the intelligence by which he is informed of the realities to which he must adjust his life. Moral law stands for a reality that rays itself into view in the human reason whether men will or not. The intuitions of it do not come at the call, or desire, or even at the consent of man. The law revealed stands independent of the individual's personality or choices and asserts itself over him. While this is true of the law revealed, the perception of the law becomes a necessity with the moral agent that is normally endowed and developed. Man does not furnish the moral law to himself. He is not the giver of it, but the recipient. The conscience, therefore, is an open window of our being, through which the objective law of righteousness to which the Creator has adjusted our nature and the constitution of the universe may be discerned by us, a sphere of reality enfolding us, with which our freedom is to harmonize our conduct. Francis Newman has admirably marked the position of this conscience-power in our constitution:

"This energy of life within is ours, yet it is not we.
It is in us, belongs to us, yet we cannot control it,
It acts without our bidding, and when we do not think of it,
Nor will it cease its acting at our command, or otherwise obey us,
But while it recalls from evil, and reproaches us for evil,
And is not silenced by our effort, surely it is not *we*;
Yet it pervades mankind, as one life pervades the trees."

The reason of these intuitions of the conscience is that back of it and around it and above it is a realm of moral obligations which must, without contingency, be made known to us, that we may order our lives aright.

Erroneous Theory

6. It is proper at this place to express dissent from some forms of theory which are at variance with the truth thus brought to light. Almost all of them are the outcome of the philosophical phenomenalism of which Kant's Critique of Pure Reason is the best illustration. It discredits the competency of our cognitive faculties to reach knowledge of things as they really are. We can know, it is said, only phenomena, while the noumena or things in themselves are incognizable; and doubt is raised whether there is a reality corresponding to what our faculties report. It is suggested that the data of these faculties, especially in the forms of intuition and universal judgments, may be mere "forms of thought," forms of knowing but not of real being, created within as well as by the mind itself, and projected thence in connection with apprehended phenomena. They may be mental fictions in whole or in part, in which the ideal must not be held as standing for actual being. Thus while time and space are necessary "forms of thought" under which all bodies and events must be known, yet time and space, it is alleged, may be but subjective forms given to the phenomena by and in the cognitive action. We are obliged, indeed, it is conceded, in practical life to follow the guidance of our necessary forms of thought. But the knowledge is merely regulative for present activity; and being a product created and shaped largely by the particular organization of our minds, this merely relative and regulative perception of truth may be different in other minds or be hereafter so changed as to present changed phenomena, superseding the judgments now given by other judgments under other views. When the adherents of the Positive Philosophy proceed to define matter as merely "a permanent possibility of sensations," faith in the reliability of our knowledge of the realities about us, as true for those realities, is thoroughly undermined. This tendency toward an invalidating of our knowledge as real for objective truth, has been fostered by recent physiological psychology which, under materialistic implications, magnifies the effect of the physical organization and condition upon the mental products. In these ways extreme idealism and positive materialism join hands in effort to reduce to uncertainty or illusion what our cognitive faculties perceive of reality and truth in both the material and moral systems about us.

But ethical science, in harmony with the soundest and best sustained philosophy of the Christian centuries, rejects these agnostic suggestions, as not only unproved but untenable. They form a theory of our intellectual faculties which cuts away the foundations of all knowledge, even of that which is most clear, fixed, necessary and unchangeable in the intelligence of the race. The theory becomes intellectual suicide, as it nullifies the real validity of all the fundamental perceptions of both sense and reason, on which its own conclusion rests. Its suggestions discredit themselves by confessing that their own foundation is but a part of the illusory, phantasmal action of faculties which, instead of perceiving what is, present but forms which they produce. While it is conceded that, even on this agnostic basis, the conscience would still possess "regulative" authority—as it still asserts its imperative "ought" for life—yet rational ethics, like self-respecting philosophy, must not vacate for our cognitive faculties the great function of knowing while attempting to exercise it, nor fail to maintain that they have been organized for real knowledge, within the sphere and measure opened to them, of the genuine realities with which we have to do, in both the material and moral worlds. The conscience, therefore, must be held, not as formative of its peculiar phenomena, but perceptive of the ethical realities of right and obligation.

Consistent with Theistic Evolution

7. It is proper also to point out here that this view of the nature of the conscience is not necessarily affected by the question of its evolutionary origin. Should the theory of man's derivative origin, under some form of theistic and teleological evolution, ever pass from its position as an hypothesis into that of scientific truth, this would not require us essentially to alter our account of the nature of this faculty. For the nature of the faculty has not been found in considerations of the mode of its origin, but from analysis of the elemental facts in its action. The adherents of the evolution hypothesis have, indeed, found one of their most formidable difficulties in attempting a satisfactory explanation of a possible origination of this faculty in the assumed forces and

laws of evolutionary action. Keeping in view the fact that the very center of the conscience-function appears in regulation and often in denial of inherited feelings and habits, the difficulty of attributing its creation to hereditary action is clearly seen and deeply felt. It has been well pointed out that "the injunctions of conscience do not run with the stream of our hereditary tendencies, but rather against them." That a law of the work and victory of hereditary forces should issue in organizing an endowment for control and repression of hereditary tendencies, seems to involve too much of a contradiction to be accepted. That the survival of the strongest in the battle of individual existence, the reign of "tooth and talon," should gradually create a faculty for asserting the obligation and law of love and kindness to the weak, fails to come properly under our conception of the working of cause and effect. Even in the theistic form of the theory, in which evolution offers itself as presenting not the cause but only the mode of creation, it is hard to conceive of the adaptation of such a process for the production of such a result—a result standing apart from the means by a total difference in both their nature and direction. It is as if the flow of the stream should create the principle of repression of flowing. The actual attempts of evolutionist writers to construct an ethical view which shall explain the phenomena of conscience and justify its authority, has added further evidence of the difficulty on this point. No such attempts have thus far been satisfactory. But the nature of the conscience, as has already been shown, is properly settled, not by the mode of its origin, but by an examination of its actual psychology and intrinsic powers. If this makes it clear, as it unquestionably does, that it is primarily intellectual and percipient in its function, then any failure of evolution or any other theory to explain its origin must much rather discredit the theory than disprove the nature of the endowment which stands as a fact. But an origin of the conscience by evolution, should it ever be proved, would introduce no trouble at this point in the science of ethics. For the faculty is competent for its office in virtue of what it is, and not by the mode through which the divine creative power worked in its formation. The necessity in the case would be met should the evolutionary mode be shown to be capable of evolving an intellectual endowment high enough in perceptive power to discern the ethical distinctions and bind their obligations on men.

CHAPTER V

THE SUPREMACY OF CONSCIENCE

By the supremacy of conscience is meant its right to exercise moral control. It expresses its proper authority. This authority is not to be thought of as original or independent, but as resting on and revealing the absolute authority of God, who has constituted the moral relations of the world and has set the conscience, with its discerning and regulative function, in the human soul. The question involved is not the right of one merely subjective faculty to impose obligation on another faculty or on all the human capacities and powers—one part of the personal self playing the role of sovereign over the other parts. This would be a shallow and misleading notion of this authority. The whole conception of the conscience is theistic, and implies, as it also testifies to, an absolute law of righteousness over all the world, established by Him who is creator and sovereign of all. It is in the discernment of this principle of rightness, with its demand for obedience to it, that the conscience comes into its position of authority and its authority becomes *de jure* supreme.

1. But the proof that such authority rightly belongs to it needs to be more fully exhibited. It is explained and made unquestionable in the following facts:

Its Sphere of Judgments

(1) It is involved in the very sphere of its discernments. This sphere is the sphere of right and duty, which, by very conception, subordinate everything else. Its primary perception is of "the

right," as having claim on every rational free agent—and then of obligation which immediately presses its moral requirement into the presence of our capacity for conformity to it. There is, indeed, a degree of authority belonging to each and all the psychical faculties, in the functions they fulfil for the direction and welfare of life. But the peculiarity of the conscience is that the realm of its functions and direction is higher than that of the other powers, the realm in which manhood reaches its supreme purpose and worth. Moral goodness, excellence of character, is the summit of the ascent to which human nature is adapted. In this our nature reaches the "supreme" and all-inclusive "good," compared with which all things else are of inferior claim and merit. The authority of the conscience, as a faculty, is thus identified with the supremacy which belongs to the idea of the morally right, of obligation, duty, the irrepealable "ought" for the conduct of life.

Shown by Nature of Action

(2) This is more distinctly apparent when we recall the nature of its action. Psychologically, the conscience does not stand as a thing of our own personal will, or as in any way making the obligation which it presents. When we examine it, as it appears in our consciousness, its movement is in the form of a necessary perception of an obligation that is upon us irrespective of our will, a law of duty not of our own framing, but imposing itself on us and demanding the homage of our will. Its possesses its authority, therefore, in the fact that it is the discernment of something higher than our will or ourselves, a principle transcending our personality and appearing as supreme law for our life and conduct. And the law connotes a lawgiver and a judge. The conscience thus puts us in the presence of One who has sovereign and absolute right to rule in us and over us. It thus becomes authoritative by its being the power or faculty through which is made known to us the principle or law of righteousness which God has established for the moral order of the world.

The Contrary is Absurd

(3) These facts, at once psychologically and metaphysically well certified, would themselves be sufficient to explain and vindicate the peculiar right of supremacy almost universally conceded to belong to the moral sense. But the proof, thus given, is confirmed by the fact that the contrary conclusion involves a manifest absurdity.

In the first place, it is incredible to suppose that man, as an intelligent, rational, free agent, capable of character, should have no provision in his mental make-up, no faculty of knowledge, furnishing a principle of guidance for meeting the responsibilities of life. For, such an absence of endowment for this purpose, would necessarily mean, either that responsibility is an illusion, a conclusion belied by the hard fact that the organization of human life inexorably treats and exacts it as real, or that man's nature is constructed in a falsehood, being bound to a high task for which it contains no endowment. Somewhere, therefore, among the human faculties, must appear a power or complex of powers whose disclosures or impulses shall furnish a rightful principle of control. To say that there is no rightful principle—that the morally good has no more right than the morally bad—would be not only absurd to reason, but fly in the face of the spontaneous and ineradicable sense of mankind, which makes the moral distinction.

Further: While the authority for self-control, to meet the ethical task and responsibilities of life, must thus be found somewhere in man's constitution, careful consideration makes it also clear that the right of supremacy cannot be attributed to any other capacity, function or impulse of our nature. The well known *argumentum ad absurdum* is fully applicable here.

Besides the conscience itself, the only other motive-forces for conduct are the physiological appetites, the desires for enjoyment, and the benevolent affections. The right of supreme control cannot be supposed to belong to the physical appetites and passions. The supremacy of these would be subversive of character and deadly to personal and social welfare. This is not simply the judgment of reason, but a fact attested by the most melancholy experiences in which blight and woe have fallen on men. Nor can the right of ruling authority belong to the desire of enjoyment. When this dominates it becomes the reign of selfishness, which, according to the consent of mankind, is utterly inconsistent with the development of noble character, or the discharge of those inter-human duties on which both individual and social well-being depends. It forms the soul of anarchy, in which the family, society, and the state would be dissolved. The true excellence and happiness of man would be impossible. The rulership of this class of motive forces is thus inconsistent with the highest and best ends to which his nature has been correlated.

Nor can the supremacy belong to the benevolent affections. These, summed up in the word love, are indeed very high and must be regarded as among the worthiest and best elements of character and principles of action. "God is love," and so near does love come to being the very essence of virtue, that it is declared to be "the fulfilling of the law." But the "love" that God is said to be is not alone in His character, nor does it rule without regard to holiness, justice, purity, or righteousness. It cannot be conceived as subordinating these to a desire to make creatures happy. On the other hand we are obliged to think of love as able to confer its favors only in accordance with the principle of righteousness. Even in its supreme exhibition, in the salvation of men, in giving its gifts, it could only act through a way that declared the divine righteousness while granting forgiveness to those that repent and forsake wrong. In human life, the love that in its own degree and order helps to the fulfillment of the law is not alone, or unregulated, or superior to the principle of duty, of truth, purity and holiness. It cannot get above these, but is itself right only when it holds its ends, of making its objects happy, in subordination to what is morally good. We must remind ourselves exactly what the supremacy of the benevolent affections would mean. Unless guided in the action through which they reach their object, they would subject everything to their own ends and take no account of the character of the ways and means, as right or wrong. As unregulated love they would lack an essential element for the office of moral control. If it be true, as it unquestionably is, that some things are wrong, no matter how lovingly they may be done, the benevolent affections cannot be the supreme guide for even the loving activities of life.

Blind affection may run, as it does in thousands of relations and instances into the widest departures from good character and into gross vices. However high the benevolent feeling may be as a motive, all its purposes and the activities through which these purposes are accomplished need the guidance of the law of righteousness, if they are to be maintained in harmony with essential virtue, holy character and human welfare. Their function must therefore be held subordinate to the authority of conscience as the capacity through which the law of rectitude, with its obligation, is presented and kept before the mental view. This conclusion does not remove love from its high position, at the very summit of things that are right and good and essential for character. It allows it to stand, as it does all other springs of action, in its full rights and value among human motives and virtues in determining duty in conduct. But it is the conscience, and not love itself, that judges and decides the obligation to it and the high rank that ought to be given it as an element of character. Thus the regulative function, even for benevolence, belongs to the ethical sense, through perception of what sentiments and acts are right in conduct. And so the peculiar business of the conscience is to watch all the forces of our nature and keep each in its place.

The view which gives the right of moral control to the conscience is thus vindicated by the plain fact that there is no other faculty or spring of action in the human constitution adapted to this function, so unquestionably requisite for the order and welfare of life.

Difficulties

2. An apparent difficulty, however, arises in connection with this conclusion. It calls for a brief consideration, lest it should be thought to form a refutation of the correctness of our view:

It comes from the acknowledged fallibility of the conscience. This seems, at first sight, inconsistent with a right to such ruling authority. If its discernment of duty in particular relations may not be fully clear and is liable to be misled, how can it be justly regarded as having this authoritative office? If its applicatory judgments are often found erroneous and need to be revised and superseded by better judgments, can we fairly hold it as charged with such regulative function? In different men, as already stated, it exhibits differing and even conflicting directions. In different nations and times its indications of duty fail to agree. Advance in civilization, knowledge and culture is marked by higher ethical standards, modifying, if not reversing, former judgments. But this large fact, so unquestionable and, apparently, so formidable, becomes, when analyzed, easily reconcilable with the position of authority given to the conscience-discernments and imperatives. For a faculty may be highest in human nature, and yet, like every other capacity, limited. Its functional action may be comparatively undeveloped, or may be strengthened and clarified. In its applicatory judgments, for fixing the ethical law of right in all the varied and complex relations and conditions of human life, it is dependent on all the subordinate faculties for the requisite light. Whatever limitations may rest on its ability, whatever partialness may mark its development, whatever complications may perplex it in adjusting duty to all the actual situations in human life, it yet remains the faculty through which the law of duty is disclosed to view, and if duty is not indicated through it, it is not indicated through any human insight at all. But no faculty loses its own particular special authority in its own place by its natural limitations and liability to error. Authority must not be confounded with infallibility. Despite its fallibility every faculty of the soul carries the authority for its own psychical office—the intellect for knowledge, the sensibility for feeling, the will for choices. The sense-perception has decisive authority for phenomena about us, the logical faculty for just conclusions from given data, the memory for recall of past experiences, the intuitional reason for axiomatic truths and first principles. If the liability to error in the psychic functions and their application to the myriad conditions in which their immediate data are used, does not vacate their place of authority in their spheres, no more does the similar liability vacate the unique authority of the conscience, which it has by its action in the supreme realm of the right and of moral obligation. Its position of authority in its sphere remains, and remains supreme, because the sphere of its action and discernments is, as pointed out, the supreme sphere of eternal righteousness and obligation.

But a further question arises at this point. If it is sometimes in error and, like an imperfect watch, gives an incorrect indication, should the conscience always be followed? Does not this fact, if it does not wholly take away its right to supremacy, at least modify the positiveness of our duty to follow its dictates? This has sometimes been a perplexing casuistic question. But the perplexity arises from failure to keep in mind the precise points involved in the problem, and to take account of the whole process through which particular duties become apparent and obligatory. Since the decision of the conscience, when rightly and fully reached, is, at the time it is given and as to the point it decides, the soul's conviction as to what is right and duty, to violate or disregard it becomes necessarily the very essence of the immoral spirit and conduct. To go contrary to what the soul sees as duty, through the only capacity it has for knowing it, is essentially moral rottenness. Whewell's statement: "To disobey the commands and prohibitions of conscience, under any circumstances, is utterly immoral: it is the very essence of immorality," is hardly too emphatic. To some writers this has seemed extravagant, in view of the fact that some of the greatest wrongs and foulest crimes of history, such as the burning of Latimer and Ridley, the St. Bartholomew massacre, the gunpowder plot, might be palliated or even justified under the plea of conscientiousness in the perpetrators. But the reconciliation of this seeming conflict between conscience and real duty is made plain by remembering two things:

First, that the conscience, being a complex faculty or power, its particular judgments of duty in particular cases, being judgments of application of the principle of rightness, are reached often through very complex processes, in which the obscuration of imperfect information, or misconception of the relations involved, or the misleading effect of prejudice created by wrong training, or some falsely imagined divine authority, may leave not only a state of doubt as to duty, but throw the decision into error. Examples of the process occur in daily experience. A question of duty is presented. We come to it with sincere, honest mind, and study it by taking into consideration all the facts and relations concerned. We get all the light we can, and we decide what the moral principle requires of us. This is the course that fair dealing with ourselves and duty requires us to pursue. But suppose that, after all this, in the fallibility of the applicatory judgments, we are thus led to do the very thing that "ought not" to be done, and violate instead of fulfil the duty which the actual relations call for from us. The following of conscience may thus have put "wrong" conduct, objectively viewed, in place of the "right" conduct which was due from us in the case. The deed, in its external form and bearing, may have been unfitting and one that ought not to have been done. But this is not the whole view or full account of the matter. For though, while in obeying our fallible conscience, we have thus failed to bring our whole outward action in the case into harmony with full duty, or have even done what to others about us or to God above us was wrong, we have maintained our own subjective personal moral integrity, in maintaining that which is the fundamental and essential element of all morality, the right intention and effort. This is the prime and the grandest element of all moral character, and is itself more than "four-fifths of conduct." There is such a thing as being innocent even when we have done what, viewed objectively, ought not to have been done. The aim, in genuine integrity of moral purpose, was to do right. The deed was a mistake. The moral status in which we may thus be placed as a result of following our conscience, is, ethically, at the opposite pole from that which we make ours when we disregard duty as fixed for us in and by our own moral judgments. This is disobedience to obligations as perceived and felt—an attitude in its nature immoral.

Secondly, the crimes and wrongs often attributed to obeying the conscience are, probably, not fairly credited to the action of conscience at all. We must distinguish what men, even conscientious men, have done or do in the name of conscience, and what the moral judgment itself has pointed out and urged as duty. It is safe to affirm that nearly all these crimes have come not by the light and dictates of the conscience, but by its suppression. There are, as all history, observation and experience testify, many other strong and bad motive-forces in human nature. The appetites and passions, the lusts of ambition, the desire of wealth and power, the striving for place and fame, the willfulness of selfishness and prejudice, are forever suggesting their objects, filling the soul with their varied and plausible pleadings, until life is driven hither and thither under the restless forces. In some men these forces hardly allow any place for the conscience to act. Not from the intuition of the moral sense or the force of conscience, but from the suggestion and direction of other motives, come the crimes that are credited to zeal inspired by conscience. Conscience is not at the helm in this business. The wrongs are a result of failure to consult its dictates—of the force and direction of other elements and tendencies of action in human nature. It was not conscience that burnt Latimer and Ridley, but intolerant fanatical hate, hot passion ruling the hour. It was not conscience that made St. Bartholomew's day full of cruelty, blood and horror, but prejudice, hatred, the unreasoning rush of excited passions. It may, indeed, seem plausible to say "that day was made by the Church's conscience asserting the duty of repressing or overthrowing heresy." And it is conceivable that that conscience should testify against the evil of heresy, and the duty of endeavoring to overcome it. But the suggestion of torture, blood and slaughter as the means of such repression, was not the work of conscience. Its guidance was thrust aside in that conduct. For this use of violence, cruelty and murder, with all their repulsive horrors, conscience did not give the command, even as God did not.

The truth with respect to the authority of conscience may be summed up as its right to control our lives in all things involving moral quality or character. Specifically: (1) In the regulation of our physical appetencies; (2) In the use to which we put our intellectual endowments and capacities; (3) In the direction and relations in which we use our emotional and affectional capacities, embracing our natural disposition, desires and aims; (4) In deciding our choices or the way we use our power of free self-determination, covering our intentions and aims; and (5) In the use we make of our capacities for physical action by which thought, feeling and the preferences of choice are turned into conduct which either fulfils or violates the duties which are evolved by our relations to being around us or above us.

The authority of conscience touches at each and all of these different points, because at each and all human life is taking shape in moral character, as either conformed to duty or variant from it. Our personal life is, in its deepest reality, a single self-conscious unit, and the action of all its capacities and powers needs to be rhythmically adjusted to the morally good. But the imperative of the conscience addresses itself pre-eminently and peculiarly to the will, or the personal self as free in choosing, and thus capable of directing and using all the personal capacities and functions. It is upon the self as free-will, as the self-determining and directive power, that the responsibility for the conduct of life is thrown, and through it, if at all, the responsibility is to be met.

And this authority becomes supreme not by any arbitrary right of one subjective faculty over another or over all the rest, but from the fact of the supremacy of what the conscience discerns and discloses, the authority of right over wrong, the obligation to eternal righteousness. Righteousness is king.

CHAPTER VI

MORAL AGENCY

Our consideration of the great truth of the distinction between right and wrong which marks human life in all ages and places, and of the existence and nature of the moral faculty discerning and enforcing this distinction, leads up to an inquiry into the aggregate complex of endowments which are essential to moral agency. The great fact of moral agency is implied and made certain in what has already been brought into view. But the presupposition of such moral agency is manifestly the moral agent, with all the requisite endowments for the sublime reality of ethical life. What are the constituents of the moral nature, in which man rises to the lofty grade of moral agency?

There are two special reasons for examining and fixing the truth on this point. First, it is needful in order to complete the scientific ethical view. Such view must be comprehensive enough to include the sum total of the powers or faculties concerned in living the moral life. The view remains faulty if any parts or features of the actual constitution are omitted or their relations to each other and to the whole are misconceived. Secondly, false and confusing representations have often been made on this point. For instance, because all the moral life moves so closely about the conscience there has been a tendency to think of the conscience and the moral nature as the same. In the eighth edition of the Encyclopædia Britannica, Dr. Alexander taught: "The moral nature of man is summed up in the word conscience. Moral nature and conscience are two names for the same thing. An analysis of conscience, therefore, will unfold man's moral nature." This resolves the whole of our moral nature into this one particular faculty. A full and correct statement must make it embrace much more. Though the conscience may be the culminating thing, it is by no means all that is requisite to endow a being with the capacities necessary for moral agency.

The truth of this is easily made clear. It is self-evident that all the essentials for moral action must be embraced in the moral nature. Some of these, manifestly, are not identical with the faculty of conscience, however closely allied to it they may be. For example, the general function of knowing is not the same as the conscience, yet it is necessary to moral action. The faculty of choice is not itself conscience or a part of conscience. Still moral action is impossible without it. Some of these essential elemental functions may in themselves possess no moral character whatever. For instance, "to know" is not itself a moral act, yet it is necessary for moral agency. The faculty of feeling is not *per se* moral. The emotions arise necessarily or at least spontaneously from acts of knowledge, and may be neither meritorious nor blameworthy. Yet the emotional function, through which thought passes into action and conduct, is involved in meeting the obligations of life. Thus it becomes plainly evident that besides the conscience by which the ethical quality and obligation are perceived, other powers by which conduct may be conformed to this obligation are requisite to fit beings for the responsibilities of moral agency. In other words, our moral nature is not only the conscience by which we approve and condemn, but also all the other endowments by which we originate or work out what is approvable or condemnable. Illustrations of this appear in our lives every day. Conscience does not love, yet love of what is good is a moral act or temper. Conscience does not care for the sick or feed the hungry, yet such charities are acts of the moral life.

We must, therefore, mark the constituents which together form man's moral constitution.

Rational Intelligence

1. The first and fundamental thing, unquestionably, is his rational intelligence. A being incapable of knowledge is incapable of the idea or sense of duty. In a world in which creative production should present no creature able to know or think, there could be no moral agency whatever. Between rocks and trees and irrational living organisms no moral relations can exist nor duties be developed. Rational intelligence, which is the basal reality of personality, is the first essential for moral agency. And this must be understood to mean the whole intellectual endowment, embracing self-consciousness, perception, memory, imagination, intuitional insight, and the varied powers of reflection and the discursive understanding. Since, as will hereafter appear (Chapter IX), duties are developed by the relations in which men stand in the system of which they are made to form a part, a knowledge of themselves and of their relations is clearly essential to a discharge of these duties. Their very constitution carries also an adaptation to an end which they must know, in order to meet their duty to themselves and others.

This dependence of ethical life upon knowledge makes itself impressively clear in the experiences and course of common life and the lessons of history. While the absence of rational intelligence, as in the case of idiocy, annuls all possibility of character and responsibility, the lower the grade of men and races in mental development, the poorer is their equipment for the demands of the full ethical standard of conduct. It is almost axiomatic that we should not look for as high grade of moral ideals and rules among ignorant people and savage tribes as in the life of intelligent civilizations. Though the principle of duty is not always turned into character in proportion to the measure of mental development and secular culture, yet experience and history affirm a clear tendency in increased knowledge to bring better sense of obligation and more prevalent rectitude of life. So well established is the recognition of this relation between intelligence and conduct, that the advocates of the evolutionist origin of man with one consent represent the emergence of intelligence as conditional for the appearance of moral agency. A knowledge of one's self and of his relations to the world around him and God above him, and the destiny to which his powers appoint him, is thus fundamental in the constitution of a nature for the sphere and reality of moral life.

The Conscience

2. The conscience—resting in the general rational intelligence and rising into the peculiar discernments and judgments which mark it—is another constituent. This is universally conceded by moral philosophy. There is, therefore, need here only to recall the place and relations of this special power in the total organism of psychical powers. The conscience, in its essential perceptions and judgments, as appears from the analysis already given, is part of the rational intelligence. It designates the power and function of the intelligent *ego*, or personal self, for discernment in the sphere of right and duty—for insight into the reality of ethical law and obligation which belong to good conduct among rational, self-directing beings. It expresses, therefore, the highest ascent of the rational intelligence, where, overlooking the whole realm of existence and relations known in other forms of knowledge, it sees, and through the emotional nature, feels, how to live as life ought to be lived.

Further, while thus the summit point in the rational intelligence, the conscience employs for its perceptions and judgments the data of all the other functions of the mind. Its discernments are made in the light of all the truth which in any way illuminates the understanding. This explains why and how the conscience is educable. It is dependent on all the other intellectual powers for a knowledge of the relations of life which develop duties and in view of which every duty is to be determined and judged. The very position of the conscience, as highest of all the powers of the intelligence, makes it, not the most independent, but the most dependent of all. All knowledge should supply light for the right conduct of life. The clearer the light, other things being equal, the clearer and more correct will be the ethical judgments. Ignorance is a darkened atmosphere to see duty in. The advance of general civilization, the progress of knowledge, the widening of the realm of science, the supernatural information given by special divine revelation, are all, therefore, if used as they should be, factors in developing the faculty of conscience into its best ability for insight into duty and for practical morality.

Free Will

3. Free-will. The only truly satisfactory psychological account of the will is that which presents it as the soul's power of causation for choices. It is the capacity of the personal *ego* or self for real choosing or free election. As in intellectual action the soul is causal for knowing or thinking, and in the sensibility it is causal for feeling or really feels, so in will the *ego* or rational self is acting as the cause of the choices which it makes. Using the term for this capacity of the personal self to choose, the will is self-determining. It originates movement. It is creative of its own acts. It is causal of its volitions. Morality consists in deliberate self-submission to the law of rectitude. Duty must be freely chosen; and the autonomy of the will, *i. e.* of the personal self, is involved in the very conception of virtue. Freedom must, therefore, be a prime characteristic of a moral nature. The whole fabric of obligation and responsibility is built upon it. It is this, as well as rational intelligence, that lifts man above the order and ongoing of material nature and makes him amenable to the claims of right and duty. It is essential to personality and its presence or absence makes and marks the deepest difference between persons and "things." We can imagine intellectual automatism; but the most brilliant intellectuality, a coruscation of mental mechanism, without reaching up into a capacity for free choice and voluntary action, would, manifestly, not make a free agent or exalt into the high realm of ethical life. The idea of duty is inapplicable except in the sphere of freedom. Moral responsibility is inconceivable without it.

In this, more than in anything else, the whole aggregation of human endowments comes to its crown. In it man becomes, in a real sense, a supra-natural being, endowed with the lofty distinction of self-direction, self-dominion and self-rulership in the presence of the great realities of right and obligation. He becomes capable of character and answerable for his conduct, as he shapes that character and determines that conduct.

And this freedom cannot be merely the freedom of simple spontaneity or voluntariness. It must be the capacity of alternative choice. There could not be real choice without capacity and room to elect between different possibilities. It is a well known definition: "Free will is possessed when, the conditions of doing something being given, one can either do or not do it." A capacity simply to act, even though it should be through intelligence and consciousness, in a way that can have no alternative and allows no choice or option, could not open a field of personal virtue or responsibility. Where only one thing is really made possible in action, and that one possible thing is already somehow necessitated, there can be no place for choice. It presents no sphere for the exercise of election—even though the faculty of election should exist. A field of choice and the faculty of choice imply and call for each other. Both are necessary for the freedom implied in responsibility. Human responsibility rests on the possession of a real capacity to make decision between real alternatives. Without these there could be no more place for morality among men than there is among the atoms or molecules of the chemical elements in their behavior in the laboratory.

The proof of free-will, in this sense, might be left to rest upon the fact that it is a necessary pre-supposition to the very conception of morality and of actual accountability. This accountability, recognized in conscience and exacted by the constitution of the world, is an omnipresent and inerasable reality. So must free-will also be. Freedom is part of the moral idea, and the idea falls apart and lapses into contradiction and confusion without it. The same necessity that obliges us to accept the truth of morality itself, obliges us to assert free-will as an attribute of a moral nature and a condition of moral agency.

But the truth of freedom is sustained by other proofs. It is proper to recall and fix clearly in mind several of these.

(1) The testimony of consciousness. This is clear and explicit. We are directly conscious of free choice. And there can be no evidence more immediate and authoritative than that of consciousness. It is the form of evidence in which all psychical

facts, activities, powers, and laws, are made known and stand certified in our knowledge. It is the certifying element for both the form and reality of all our knowing. It is that in which we "know that we know," and without which there can be no knowledge. It is, therefore, the foundation certitude. Our systems of science, our conclusions in philosophy, our intuitions into first truths and laws, and all the confidence with which we accept truth in all these great realms of mental life, rest back on the observations, reasonings and conclusions for whose reality and order consciousness is our most fundamental voucher. To its tests and verifications all the processes of knowing must submit. No truth is even visible except in the light in which consciousness holds all our acts and forms of intelligence. No form of our knowing can be surer than this. To discredit it is to discredit that without whose help not a step in knowledge can be taken. Upon this fundamental and unsurpassable evidence rests the great fact of free-will. No person, in the simple light of his unperverted and unperplexed consciousness, doubts his free-will. He finds himself in exercise and use of it every day and every hour. He knows himself to be perpetually making decisions within his own liberty, if he knows anything. The witness to it is direct, and he holds himself, and others hold him, responsible for his choices and the deeds he does in carrying them out. He deliberately and consciously elects his way through clearly seen open alternative possibilities. If he is to believe that in reality he does not do so, he must believe that his consciousness is a perpetual fraud upon him. But thus the authority for the reality of all his psychical capacities and acts is overthrown, and he does not "know that he knows" in any of his knowing.

It is not a sufficient answer to all this, when it is said that in this way of proof we are making the testimony of consciousness reach further than it actually does. Some psychologies undertake to limit consciousness to a disclosure of simply the actual volition, or other psychical acts, and not of acts or volitions which we imagine might have been but were not. Thus, it is said, the proof of another possible choice, as an alternative to that of the actual volition, fails to be covered by the consciousness. The supposed act is outside of its reach of purview and testimony. But such a psychology is untrue to the full deliverance of the consciousness. A just and full account of it, as is clearly seen in our experience, must hold it as covering not only the act of choice, but the *power to choose*. The human consciousness is a self-consciousness, and in it we truly know the personal self as the power for the various forms of activity which it reveals. Not more truly are we conscious of the power really to think or feel than really to choose, among diverse possibilities. We have direct knowledge of the power of electing in the very act of election. And thus, not only the untutored consciousness, but one trained to the sharpest and deepest self-inspection, will be found a full witness to freewill as a capacity of alternative choice.

(2) The implications of the natural constitution of the world. Mankind are in fact framed into and held under the principle of freedom. The whole system of which man forms a part answers to the testimony of consciousness. Bishop Butler, in his immortal Analogy, has shown with resistless clearness and force that in the constitutional organism of society and the experiences of actual life free-will is assumed for human nature. Both by natural and moral law men are governed as free agents. The physical order of the earth, as a place where bodily and moral welfare are conditioned on obedience to discoverable relations and principles, pre-supposes human intelligence and liberty. Nature in her ongoings requires every individual to adjust himself carefully to its laws of health, safety and happiness. There is an incessant appeal to him to use his intelligence and liberty in accordance with the demands of his ever-changing conditions and relations in life. The idea that everything takes place by necessity is not only at variance with his sense of freedom, but is found utterly inapplicable in practical living. A youth, if such a case be supposed, trained under the notion that he must not be held responsible for his acts, since they take place by necessity, would soon find his dream of irresponsibility disturbed and disallowed. At every turn he would find the inexorable forces of nature and society refusing to recognize his claim. Government, law, administration, all the various functions through which human affairs are held together in orderly movement, assume the individual's power and obligation to determine his conduct and

hold him chargeable with consequences. Though supposed speculatively true, the doctrine proves false in practice. It is in fact untrue to the constitution of human life. "The thing here insisted on," says Butler, "is that under the present natural government of the world we find ourselves treated and dealt with as if we were free, prior to all consideration whether we are or not. Were this opinion, therefore, of necessity admitted to be ever so true, yet such is in fact our condition and the natural course of things, that whenever we apply it to life and practice, this application of it always misleads us, and cannot but mislead us, in a most dreadful manner, with regard to our present interests." Beyond all question, as is evident to every thoughtful person, mankind deal one with another on the pre-supposition and principle of freedom, and of the responsibility which is ethically unthinkable except on that freedom. Personal, social, and governmental relations are framed upon this principle, and are a perpetual expression of it. Men universally treat each other—and under the actual inter-relations of life cannot but treat each other—as free beings, The inference is direct and necessary that they are such, unless we concede that human life is organized into a necessary order of living that is false to their real nature and unjust in its penalties.

(3) It is to be further noted that while freedom rests thus on the direct and positive evidence of consciousness and the actual order of life, the contrary doctrine of necessity or determinism arises only from assumptions or implications of speculative thought. This is a fact that needs to be clearly and fully fixed in mind. Necessitarianism is without any direct witness of consciousness, and is not forced or even suggested by the natural sense of mankind. It is not required as a working theory for the business or natural conduct of life. It is only a product of speculation or ideal theorizing. It is constructed from different standpoints of thought. In some speculation it rests simply on certain ontological assumptions, sometimes pantheistic as in Spinozism, sometimes materialistic as in non-theistic evolutionism. In both these cases freedom disappears in the absoluteness with which the substance of the universe unfolds into all its products and manifestations. In some other

speculations it appears as a conclusion from certain metaphysical views of the law of causation and its supposed application in the realm of psychical activity. In this form of theory every volition is viewed as standing in the relation of a mere effect to a cause which determines the will to it, in fixed connection and force of antecedence and consequence. The volition comes, it is represented, as the necessary result—not as a real choice by self-determining personality, but produced by environment, mental structure, and disposition. Not the *ego* or personal self, as free spirit endowed with capacity for real election, but the environment, motives, and disposition decide and fix the volition for the person, which by an illusion of consciousness appears as done by himself. In still other speculation necessitarianism comes as an inference from conceptions formed as to the divine sovereignty and the absoluteness with which it must direct creature movement. The doctrine thus has its plausibility, not from the conscious working of the human mind or the natural order of conduct and welfare, but as theoretical conclusions from certain forms of speculative thinking. It is therefore the product of metaphysical theorizing. It is not a datum of pure psychology. It is not taught by life. It is not known as a fact. It is not called for by the practical needs of daily self-direction. It has only secondary forms of suggestion and support—the precarious evidence from special theorizing in ontology and metaphysics. And it introduces more difficulties than it shuts off, while it collides with the moral consciousness of mankind and its sense of responsibility for conduct and the formation of character. In the light of these truths it ought not to be regarded as having any validity. It is surely incredible that the doctrine of necessity should be true when the actual constitution of human life, in all its personal, social, and governmental relations, requires us to treat it as false, being practically inapplicable. Utterly beyond belief is it that while the inexorable necessities of daily behavior bind us to the principle of freedom and responsibility, there should be in the real constitution of the world no actual freedom in deciding on choices or determining our conduct. Moral agency must be free agency, in open alternatives of choice. It involves both the subjective capacity to choose and a realm for its exercise in diverse possibilities.

Sensibility and Actions

4. Powers of sensibility and action, by which the dictates of conscience may be turned into actual conduct and character, complete the moral constitution.

(1) It has already been seen (pages 44–47) that in the complex action of the conscience itself the sensibility is awakened in the form of emotion, as a feeling of obligation arising from a perception of obligation. This has already shown the sensibility to be a part of the moral organization. Conscience itself includes emotion. Duty perceived becomes duty felt, if the moral life is normal; and the feeling is motive-force for the choice and the fulfillment of duty. Emotional powers are thus constituent in the structure of man's moral nature. The moral emotions are occasions for ethical choices and deeds.

(2) But, further, the movements of the sensibilities are themselves either morally good or evil, and form a sphere of personal life to which moral quality belongs. Man's affections and desires, his loves and hatreds, his enjoyments and aversions, constitute a domain where the ethical distinctions are to be applied. They hold and exhibit elements of character. We may not, indeed, say that a being of pure intellect, void of all emotion, would be utterly incapable of character and irresponsible, but we are compelled to think that the moral life in such case would be without what forms the highest ethical excellence and glory of character, viz.: love, benevolence, delight in righteousness and joy in pure affection. The regulation of the affections and passions, the purification of the inmost "thoughts" of what the sacred scriptures call "the heart" is vital to right character. The capacity to love is an equipment for the moral life. It is virtuous to love what ought to be loved. The capacity to hate is also such an equipment—the obligation being to hate what ought to be hated as morally wrong. Benevolence may not be, as some have contended it is, the essence or ground of all virtue, but, unquestionably, it is a virtue of highest rank, and the capacity for

it is a prominent element in man's moral organization. The same is true of the whole emotional and affectional capacity in the human soul. It is part of the constitution for true character and life.

(3) Still further, man's powers of action, in which the ethical distinctions and choices are wrought out into their proper deeds, are part of his organization for the true moralities of life. However deeply the foundations of ethics may be laid in personal individuality, the ethical life concerns more than self, and finds its largest field in inter-human relations. Human solidarity is as real as human individuality. Humanity is an organism, in which each person has his place and mission. The individual's sphere of duty is not simply his own soul, but the broad reach of all his relations to the world about him, in which duties are developed and right conduct is required. In all this wide sphere obligation can be met only through his endowment with power to carry into effect, in action, his moral judgments and convictions of right. Moral science must consider man not merely as a knower and contemplator or lover of the right, but also as a doer of it in righteous deeds. Hence man's moral nature, as his endowment for the moral life, is not all brought under review until it is seen to include the realm of his feelings and those executive powers which turn the ethical discriminations and choices into righteous conduct.

We thus sum up the constituents of man's moral nature: intelligence, the conscience, free-will, and capacities for affection and doing. Where these are united the subject is organized for knowing duty and fulfilling it. But a final fact, of profound import, needs yet to be added, not as a further faculty, but rather as a consequence resultant from the union and coaction of these endowments, viz.: that this organism of faculties presents not simply a capacity as a possibility of the moral life, but a positive, vital motive adjustment and organic pre-disposition toward it. It is not simply framed to it as an articulation of dead timber, but is adapted to it as a complex of living forces for normal movement. The moral constitution, if not disordered or wrecked, carries thus a living trend or impulse toward knowing duty and doing it. This impulse, seemingly pervading, if not standing behind, the whole mental activity, as a sub-conscious pre-disposition, appears as an original aptitude or incorporated purpose in the total human psychical organization. Hence human nature, if normal, is not indifferent to right and wrong. Its true life is one of positive affinity for the good. If, under internal disorder or particular circumstances, counter-tendencies appear and prevail, this does not disprove [the fundamental and normal set of humanity for the moral life. Man is made for the right as he is made for God. This conception of the positiveness of his total moral organization is necessary to complete the view of man as a moral agent.

CHAPTER VII

THE REALITY OF RIGHT AND WRONG

In this chapter we pass the dividing line between the two great parts of ethics. Thus far we have considered only the facts and manifestations of our moral nature. We have traced the unquestionable phenomena of moral distinctions and obligation in human thinking, feeling, and conviction. We have found the explanation of these phenomena in the action of a faculty or complex of faculties of the human soul, that discerns and affirms these distinctions. We have studied this power and marked its data from its initial perception of the ethical distinction through its further discernments, emotions and judgments to its full assertion of moral responsibility. We have seen its unique authority explained by the supremacy of the law of right and duty which it reveals, and have noted the aggregate of endowments belonging to man's moral agency.

But the mere registry of these moral phenomena is not the full explanation of them. We must examine yet what they imply. From the faculty that perceives we must turn to look at the nature of that which is perceived. We may call the part already traversed the science of ethics, as dealing with and systematizing the facts of experience. The part that remains takes us into the metaphysics of ethics, as exhibiting the abiding verities so perceived and to which we find ourselves so responsibly related— not what is in us, but what is above and over us to which our moral consciousness corresponds. Having visited "the moral consciousness in its own home" and listened to its story of "right" and "duty" and "responsibility," we must go forth and explore the realm that answers to that story. This realm is the objective moral system to which human conduct is to be adjusted.

The precise question of this chapter is whether the distinction of right or wrong, subjectively and psychologically made, is also objectively true and real, marking an actual qualitative difference in the deeds and intentions of men, or is a mere appearance, a fiction and illusion of our own minds. Is the principle of duty a reality for right life, as something belonging to the constitution of the world, or only an idea which our minds have manufactured— only our own thought reflected back upon us, as is our face that seems so real in the mirror?

It would seem that the very asking of this question should be itself a sufficient answer. But doubt has been raised by speculative metaphysics. Hence we must examine it.

Source of Doubt

1. The doubt comes from misleading representations of the relativity of knowledge. Unquestionably there is a sense in which our knowledge may justly be said to be "relative." It is not absolute, unconditioned or unlimited. We can know only as we have facilities for knowing, and under the conditions and aspects in which objects are presented to them. We are restricted to the modes and degrees of our given capacities. There are probably many realities about us of which we can know nothing. We have no organs for their perception. Even the things that we do know reach off into transcendent relations. Philosophy has long confessed the relative character of our knowledge. Even the percepts of sense-experience, say for instance, of sight or hearing, when analyzed in physical science are found to be, in their objective cause or material conditions, somewhat different from the simple report of the organ of sense—color being the subjective sensation of light-rays on the retina of the eye, and sound the effect of vibrations of the atmosphere upon the sensorium. But in recent times various theories have represented our knowing faculties as largely untrustworthy and their data as invalid in spheres where their functions appear most certain and explicit. Locke gave basis for a movement in this direction by teaching

that the immediate objects of the mind are not things, but "ideas." Berkeley's idealism repudiated the sufficiency of sense-perception to prove the objective existence of the material world. Hume questioned the substantial existence of both matter and mind. In the view of Kant human knowledge reaches only to "phenomena," the appearance of things, while the things as they are "in themselves" cannot be known. The mind projects and imposes its own subjective forms of thought upon the universe. Sir Wm. Hamilton, Dean Mansel, J. S. Mill, Alexander Bain and Herbert Spencer have developed theories, variously modified but agreeing in this, that even our necessary forms of rational perception are not to be held as standing for more than relative truth, i. e. subjective impressions in our minds in the presence of environment. Doubt is cast upon the point whether what is true to our necessary or actual thought is also really true for the objective world.

The teaching will be best understood by several quotations. Sir Wm. Hamilton, though a natural realist, influenced by the speculations of Kant, while acknowledging an underlying reality for phenomena, taught that we can never know them except "under modifications determined by our own faculties."

J. S. Mill, going further, says: "Our knowledge of objects, and even our fancies about objects, consist in nothing but the sensations they excite, or which we imagine them exciting in ourselves ... This knowledge is merely phenomenal ... The object is known to us only in one special relation, namely, as that which produces, or is capable of producing certain impressions on our senses; and all that we really know is these impressions."

Herbert Spencer asserts the relativity of all knowledge, and says: "Clearly as we seem to know it, our apparent knowledge proves on examination to be utterly irreconcilable with itself. Ultimate religious ideas and ultimate scientific ideas, alike turn out to be merely symbols of the actual, not cognitions of it."

Plainly these theories do not make our knowledge a genuine apprehension of reality, but merely internal and unreliable mental states. It is only a subjective phenomenon. We cannot know that it stands for the real truth of things. Rather, we are told, it does not. It is but an effect within the mind, determined, it may be, by things without, but modified, if not created, by the constitution and action of the mind itself. The receiving mind, like the receiving lens, determines the shape and color of the apprehended phenomenon. If there be any reality behind it and correspondent to it, we can never assure ourselves of it. The theory thoroughly discredits the trustworthiness of our faculties, both of sense-perception and of reason. They do not report the things of the world as they really are, but merely as they affect us. Our necessary conceptions, such as time, space, beauty, cause, moral law, cannot be proved to be anything else than phenomena within us. The conclusion is well stated in the language of Mr. Grote in his explanation of the views of the Greek sophists: "As things appear to me, so they are to me; as they appear to you, so they are to you." It is altogether a subjective matter. We can have only a relative morality—not conformed to an objective and universal standard, but to the particular impressions we find within us.

Evidently this doctrine of relativity lands us in universal intellectual skepticism. It gives us agnosticism. Nothing is sure in a single department of knowledge. If our minds are forever presenting to us internal "forms of thought" that stand not really for the "forms of being" in the real world, if they are actually creating or painting for us what we seem to perceive and what appear to be realities objective to our faculties and existing independently of them, there is no possibility of reaching truth of any kind. But in the domain of morals this theory would prove peculiarly destructive. If the qualities of right and wrong be not in very truth real, if they be not verities of conduct in the constituted relations of human life, if the ideas answer not to a true distinction set before us for our recognition and conformity, then virtue is a dream, obligation an illusion, and conscience a fraud.

Over against this false we must place the true conception of the relativity of knowledge. We must hold, as the spontaneous sense of mankind and the best sustained psychology and philosophy of the centuries affirm, that our cognitive powers are genuine faculties for discerning the truth of things, that, while not infallible nor unlimited, they give us substantially correct

90

knowledge, as far as it goes, of the realities of the natural and moral world in which we are placed. These powers of intelligence are not set to act delusively and imprison us in phantasmagoria or a factitious system false to that which actually exists. The correct theory, the only one that is really rational and can be lived out, must ever be that, as far as we have faculties to know at all and use them loyally, we know what is and because it is. The true reason of our knowing is the real existence of knowable realities. Instead of knowing only appearances, we know the very things that appear—not perfectly, or without possibility of mistake, but yet truly. The end of knowledge is not to give us a phantasmagorical world for endless illusion, but the actual world, with its divine constitution and movement, in which we are to live, and with whose facts and laws, physical and moral, we are to harmonize our lives.

2. The false conception of the relativity of knowledge being thus set aside, and the psychological law, that the correlate of knowing is reality, being recognized, we are prepared to see the truth on the point of inquiry in this chapter, as follows:

Objective Reality

(1) The qualities of right and wrong, involved in the ethical distinction, are not merely subjective impressions or appearances, imposed on conduct by the human mind, but are objective, belonging to the external world of relations and action, real for apprehension and conformity. They are without us as well as within us. And they come within us because they are realities without us for us to know and observe. The moral qualities, as real features of required behavior of free beings in their given relations to each other, belong to the constitution of the world as well as to the faculties of the human mind. They are real qualities of action and motives to action whether men perceive or take note of them or not. As truly as the starry sky is above us, before we open our eyes to see it, so the principle of righteousness is established for life before we enter it or our faculties awake to discover it. The principle of moral law is framed into the constitution of the world and human life. It is back of the

discernment of it, imbedded in the demand which the constituted relations of nature make for proper behavior of free, intelligent beings. The law of duty is fixed in these relations. It abides there to be recognized and fulfilled by all beings endowed with moral perception and freedom. Moral law is a profounder and broader thing than a simple uncertain mental fiction in personal thinking. It belongs to the immense, almost infinite realm of creature inter-relations of the universe.

The reality, however, is not to be thought of as a material entity or substantive essence, but solely as a quality of the intentions and conduct demanded by and in the relations sustained by men and other moral beings. It is the reality of an established obligation. It belongs to character.

The right, as moral law, has ever been venerated as something supersensible, absolute, and divine. The early Egyptian teaching represented its home as in Deity. Buddhistic philosophy conceives of it as an imperishable dominion over gods and men. Christianity has enforced it as based in the very nature of God, and as a principle of order ordained for the whole universe of personal life and behavior. Not more real are the solid rocks of the mountain or the strong waves of the sea. Not more real for the material realm is the law of gravitation than is the law of ethical righteousness for the spiritual realm, the realm of free conduct. And the latter is superior and of higher value than the former. This truth speaks in the old apothegm: "*fiat justitia, ruat cælum.*"

Not Dependent on Organization

(2) The qualities of right and wrong in conduct are not dependent on the peculiar mental organization or temperament of the race. This results from the objectivity of the law of obligation. Only the perception of them is so dependent, while the moral qualities are abidingly real for all beings high enough in the scale of being to discern them. Just as we must believe that the sun exists as an extended body independently of our eyes or minds, and would have to be so apprehended by any inhabitant of Neptune or Jupiter endowed with capacity to perceive it as it is,

so we must believe that truth and love and kindness are right, and falsehood, injustice, malignity and ingratitude are wrong, not as made so by our peculiar personal constitution, but *per se*, in any inhabited world of the stellar heavens; and that the only subjective condition for their so appearing is the possession of the faculty for perception of moral quality.

There may, indeed, be a doubt among finite moral agents, with limited knowledge, how far a certain thing may be true or false, kind or malignant, just or unjust, but the quality of truth or falsehood, kindness or malignity, justice or injustice being perceived in it, it is impossible that such truth, kindness and justice should not be judged right and their opposites wrong. The ethical distinction, objectively viewed, is an ethical difference, perceived as such, if perceived at all.

Immutable and Eternal

(3) The moral distinctions, with the moral qualities involved, being thus objective, and not the product of a special temporary organization of the percipient, are immutable and eternal. This is involved in the very nature of the qualities themselves. By eternal necessity of what they are, justice and love must be unchangeably and forever right. They are not thus right because we think or feel them so, but we think and feel them so because they are so, because of the immutable and enduring nature of justice and love themselves. They hold and carry the kind of motive and action that ought to prevail in the relations of intelligent personal life, everywhere and in all time. So malignity, injustice, falsehood, and cruelty are wrong by the very nature of the qualities that make and mark them; and the personal intentions and conduct that hold them can never be right any more than a thing can be itself and yet other than itself.

Men's judgments as to whether particular conduct is fair or just or kind or honest, may change and do change. Different nations and ages class certain acts and ways of men very differently. But these are only judgments of application, and so only secondary ethical judgments. This has already been pointed out in Chap. IV, pp. 67–68. They depend on the degree to which the moral qualities of the conduct may be discerned amid the complicated relations and obscurities that often perplex a right understanding of it. But while men change their judgments of the justice, benevolence, or truth of particular forms of behavior, they do not change their judgments that justice, love and truth are right—necessarily and immutably so. The behests of duty are imbedded in the necessary relations of intelligent free beings. Virtue is no shifting subjective illusion, shaped by our inner mental mold. No change of the percipient's intellectual constitution can change the realities of right and wrong. No removal from world to world can change them. No distant age in eternity can reverse them, and discover virtue to be wrong or sin right, or either as without moral quality. The distinction is eternal, and no future can arrest our responsibility with respect to it. God calls us to identify ourselves with what is right and shun all wrong, as realities with which we stand in immutable, unending relation, for good or evil.

Grandeur of Moral Law

3. The truth thus reached on this point is one of exceeding importance. It brings to view the grandeur of the moral law. It shows this law to be truly transcendental, belonging not to transient material forms or physiological structure, nor to special psychical constitutions of men or races, nor organized instinct, nor subjective mental illusion, nor peculiar hereditary experience, nor transformed sense of realized or supposed utility, nor any local adventitious circumstances and training, but to the supreme supersensible realm of universal and necessary ideas and truth, in which the universe of rational thought and divine order lives and moves and has its being and welfare. In this truth, therefore, the moral law begins to appear in its true greatness and value, in its universal dominion and infinite importance. It comes down upon us with a mighty impression. It thrills us into enthusiasm. As long as the moral idea is accounted a mere product of environment and biological evolution or experienced utility, a blind hereditary instinct, an organized impulse, a fiction of education, or a temporary behest of individual or racial

organization, it is a thing of but little dignity and of limited moment. It is worthy of no more reverence than a form of protoplasm or a passing mental impression. Not reflecting an objective reality of universal, supreme and permanent validity, but only a special phenomenon of the human organization and this transient life, it can inspire but small respect. Only in the truth here reached does the authority of the moral law stand out in its majesty and illimitable range and sweep. Only in it can that law be rightly effective for the good conduct of men and the safe formation of character in the mold of immortal excellence.

Reality is Dividing Line

4. The recognition of the objective validity of the moral distinctions marks one of the chief dividing lines between true and false theories of moral philosophy. A failure to recognize this point not only leaves the point itself a blank, but usually means error both in the conception of the nature and function of conscience and of the grounds and claims of right and virtue. With respect to conscience the failure reduces it from a power of true discernment of what is, into an instinct acting blindly or a make-believe of obligation through judgments indistinguishable from those of utility, pleasure or advantage, or into a passing product of racial experience or education. So instead of explaining the unique authority of the conscience it undermines and dissolves that authority into non-moral elements. Obligation itself becomes but a synonym for an impulse toward certain forms of pleasure or advantage. As to the grounds and claims of right, these are thus caused to disappear in the non-moral elements into which right and wrong are dissolved. The ethical distinctions, the great moral phenomena of the ages, with all the interests of practical morality, instead of being explained and justified, are explained away. If, therefore, ethical theory is to exhibit the metaphysical validity of the moral consciousness of men, no view can reasonably be regarded as correct that dissipates the very reality which the conscience assumes to see and without which the moral judgments lose their rational foundations. For if the objective and transcendent character of the

ethical distinction be denied, morality necessarily drops down into, at best, a temporary biological provision for the utilities of this ephemeral life, or, at worst, into a deep fraud of our faculties, estopping the use of our freedom by a phantom bugbear of moral distinctions. If, therefore, virtue is not to be disrobed of its honor, if righteousness is not to be cast down from the supreme place which the reason of mankind has ever accorded it, if the idea of duty is not to be belittled, invalidated and overthrown, ethical theory must recognize and emphasize the objective and permanent reality of the moral law as an unchanging law of obligation and responsibility for the conduct of free agents. Otherwise the so-called ethical theory is not a theory of the ethical reality, but one that sinks the supposed ethical reality into non-moral elements and illusion. To vindicate the authority of conscience, the immutable foundations of righteousness must be maintained, not dissolved.

Relation to Evolution

5. The relation of this truth to the wide-spread hypothesis of the evolutionary origin of man dare not be ignored at this place. Frank admission has already been made that this hypothesis, as setting forth a mere mode of creation by God, does not appear to be necessarily inconsistent with the existence of conscience. Any mode that can produce a faculty of mental power capable of perceiving or making the ethical distinction, suffices on that point—though grave difficulties stand in the way of accounting for it under any evolutionist explanation thus far given. But how is it with respect to the supersensible reality of the moral law, as the reality perceived by the conscience? Can evolution account for it, or even allow any place for it?

Theistic Evolution

To these questions, the answer must be, first, that evolution, in the theistic conception, if supposed capable of developing the faculty of conscience, must also be regarded as consistent with the existence and place of the moral law. The infinite intelligence and purpose back of the creative evolution, and through it originating a power for ethical perception, must be conceded to be equally capable, in that method of forming the universe, of establishing the principle and law of duty in the relations in which rational and self-determining creatures are to live. Provided only that a rational first cause be assumed and the plan of the world be viewed as laid in aims of divine order, a moral system as well as moral agents may, surely, be created by slow advance of life no less completely than by instantaneous fiat of power. The theistic theory of evolution, assuming the cosmic system to be grounded in the will and power of God and filled with his ever-working presence does not necessarily bring any trouble into the question of fixed moral law. The moral law, resting in the same divine source whence arise the laws that are revealed in physical nature, comes into play as soon as moral agents are created in relations which call for right sentiments and conduct. The rational purpose which ordained physical laws, in necessity, for material order, ordains moral law for order of personal agents acting in freedom. The question, therefore, with respect to this kind of evolution need not embarrass the question of the reality of immutable moral law—at least when the theory of evolution is so shaped as to give its fundamental assumptions full and consistent place and force.

Atheistic Evolution

But, secondly, on the other hand, answer must be made, that under no theory of atheistic and merely materialistic and naturalistic evolution can the objective existence of moral law be logically or rationally maintained. This kind of evolutionism is not only helpless before the task of accounting for it, but logically excludes the possibility of it. For any theory that presents the cosmos as a pure naturalism of matter, or is agnostic as to an intelligent author of nature, furnishes no realm or materials for moral law. This becomes evident, beyond doubt, from the following considerations:

(1) According to the hypothesis "the potency of all things" is in matter with its energy and modes of motion. This is the "all

and the one" (τὸ πᾶν κὰι ἕν) of the universe, at once the only essence and ground of its existence and ongoing. No intelligent first cause is assumed, no creative reason to begin or determine the evolution. There is no ordering mind or purpose in it—for its origin, in the process, or as to its end. It is avowedly a purely mechanical theory of the universe—matter and force acting in self-contained energy without design. All rational, purposive, or teleological idea is wanting. Now it is evident that this pure mechanism of matter and energy must be not only without any moral element whatever, but necessarily incapable of evolving the moral. It is an infinite and endless automatism. Though it should run on æon after aeon it is still only a mechanism of atoms in eternally unfree material movement. The unmoral elements can never produce moral law; and, *ex hypothesi*, there is no intelligent free moral being behind or in the movement to create or establish moral law through it.

(2) Further, this form of evolutionism, returning, as it does, to the ancient notion of the universe as a perpetual flux, even if imagined to be able to evolve the moral out of non-moral elements, could present no permanent and stable ethical law. In such evolution, without beginning and without end, all things are only a continual becoming, "an eternal process moving on." There is and can be nothing fixed, whether of forms or relations, but only a shifting, necessitated, everlasting scene of aimless beginnings and disappearances. Could we even conceive—which we cannot, because the concept is possible only in connection with purpose and ideal order—that the ethical "ought" should momentarily appear, it would soon be broken up and passed by, like the bubble on a stream,

"A moment here, then gone forever."

Manifestly, this perpetual motion, forever changing and superseding its own forms and products, cannot be considered father to even a rational stable conscience, much less a sure abiding moral law for its steady recognition and eternally reverent regard. "The child of contingency remains contingent." And so the advocates of this empirical, materialistic, and atheistic

Milton Valentine

evolutionism consistently maintain that there is no absolute moral law, and that what seems so is only shifting hereditary judgments generated by experience and utility or some instinct formed by biological processes.

(3) But further. In this merely naturalistic evolution all the essential presuppositions of moral law are wanting and excluded. This is easily seen. (*a*) It has already been pointed out that the action of conscience is theistic, its authority arising from its perception of a law of duty imposed on it and representing a moral law-giver (See Chap. IV, py. 79–80; Chap. V, pp. 87–88). So moral law, as a rule of ethical righteousness, is necessarily theistic. It is thinkable only as a requirement made by rational intelligence for fitting conduct among personal agents. It rests in a world-system of rational ends and ideal requirements. The standard is established by intelligence. Should it be objected, that we may regard the standard as made by the mind of men only, and altogether a human and subjective thing, it is enough to remind the reader that according to the hypothesis, there is no human mind as a different entity from matter, the only "mentality" left being merely particular effects of molecular or brain activity, and therefore only successive passive products, simply revealing what, if it exists at all, must exist as the molecular matter behind them. The autocratic moral law which the conscience finds, but does not make, is conceivable therefore, only as part of intelligent ordering in a rational world-system. But according to the hypothesis no moral reason has framed or regulates the order of the physical forces that create the relations of life. (*b*) Moral law, with responsibility, is inconceivable except in connection with personal freedom in the subject of it. But in this kind of evolutionism, everything is reduced to the mechanism of matter; and its supporters agree that our personal freedom is an illusion. There can be no more morality in the thoughts, aims and conduct of men than in the digestion of food or the growth and decay of a tree.

While, therefore, theistic evolution does not present anything inconsistent with the reality and recognition of moral law, every hypothesis which exhibits the world, in its ground and processes, as the mere mechanism of material forces, stands in logical and

99

irreconcilable antagonism. This antagonism, however, is not to be taken as overthrowing or even weakening the truth set forth in this chapter. Rather, the antagonistic hypothesis, which fails in so many other respects to meet the necessities of a rational or scientific account of the phenomena of the universe, discredits itself still further by its incongruity on this great point.

CHAPTER VIII

THE GROUND OF RIGHT

This topic carries the inquiry concerning moral law one step further than that determined in the last chapter. It being settled that that law is objectively and permanently real, for the recognition of conscience, we must yet seek some explanation of the basis of the reality. Why are some things right and others wrong? What is the reason of the difference? On what is the law of right grounded? We seek the explanation of its existence and the obligation it imposes.

It must be remembered that even those who hold the moral behests to be merely subjective, products in some way of the psychological constitution, nevertheless endeavor to account for them in some relations or forces back of themselves. These accounts, as will appear, are exceedingly varied. Inasmuch, therefore, as nearly all the differing ethical theories seek to give some explanation and ground for moral obligation, the inquiry now before us presents the point about which the chief contests of moral philosophy have been waged. The different answers have been the main determinants of the different systems.

Our examination must include three things: a clear definition of the point of inquiry; some notice of the leading theories; and a positive statement of the ground as demanded by reason and the interests of moral life.

The Question Defined

I. Definition. This is necessary because it has sometimes been confounded with the question: What is the ground of obligation? We must distinguish between the "ground of right" and the "ground of obligation." The point before us is not why we are under obligation to do a right act, but why the act is right. Manifestly the rightness of the proposed action is the ground of the obligation to do it; that is, the obligation is grounded on the right. The exact inquiry is—and must be, in order to reach the real and abiding moral foundations—on what is the right, whose perception obligates, grounded? A quest after the ground of the "obligation" simply, might satisfy those who reduce conscience to a mere instinct or sentiment, and the moral standard to a mere internal product of association, education or of biological organization. To them it might seem enough to give an explanation of the felt obligation. In such case they might plausibly, as they often do, affirm that the moral bond, being thus organically insured and fixed in the moral consciousness, must remain the same, no matter what theories, even though purely materialistic, may be formed of its genesis and nature. But so soon as the ethical reality is seen in its cosmic place and transcendental character we want an explanation not only of the ground of obligation to right conduct, but also of the ground of the right which evokes the sense of obligation.

Various Theories

II. Leading Theories. We must include, in this review, both the theories which offer only an explanation of the phenomenon of obligation and those that seek an elucidation of the principle of righteousness as objective moral law. In the long continued discussion of the subject these theories have been immensely varied and modified, but the differences thus noted divide all explanations into two classes, viz., those which make the moral stand in something subjective and those that find it objective. In the cursory rehearsal of them, here needed, we will present them in chronological order, irrespective of their belonging to one class or the other, noting, however, their relation to this distinction which divides them. Such historical glance will give an outline of the development of thought on the subject, and help us to reach and appreciate the true conclusion.

Egyptian Teaching

1. Egypt's golden age was in the morning of the world's historical period, and we must look far back for its best ethical thought. With the Egyptians morality and religion were closely identified. The ethical view was united with the theological and determined by it. They, however, dealt with the subject of duty only in separate maxims and precepts, without framing a theory of obligation. But the purity and elevation of these precepts have been a wonder to many in our modern days. It is, however, easily explained. Their religion was monotheistic. God was a good and righteous Being, with power and rulership, the source of all things for man. The Egyptians connected all that was pure and good with God and recognized their dependence on Him and their duty to live according to His will. Thus their moral consciousness rose above the function of a mere subjective instinct or a feeling of responsibility to their fellow-men, and included a sense of direct amenability to divine authority. The goal of the moral endeavor, ever overcoming evil, was regarded as attained, not in this, but in a future life of blessedness under the divine approval. Their view grounded all duty objectively, and practically identified it with piety.

Chinese Teaching

2. Chinese teaching, too, was theological. The theology was essentially monotheistic, but overgrown with superstitions and idolatrous practices. It taught that man is the creature of God, and was endowed by heaven with a nature for the practice of good, a nature that, if followed properly—*i. e.* in the "golden mean"—invariably leads men aright. The path indicated by nature is the will of God concerning duty. "What heaven has conferred is called the nature; an accordance with this nature is called the path of duty; the regulation of this path is called instruction." The chief contribution to the Chinese teaching by the sage Confucius

(B. C. 551–478) was his proclamation of the principle of "reciprocity," *i. e.* doing as we would have others do to us. Though the elements of the moral problem were thus included fairly well for ordinary conduct, they were not framed into a distinct philosophy of the ground of right.

Views in India

3. India's sacred books abound in moral maxims and counsels. Brahmanism is substantially a philosophy of life rather than a religion. But its pantheism and doctrine of the pre-existence and transmigration of souls have distorted and misdirected the moral idea. Its pantheism confounds the human with the divine, both in its origin and destination. Its belief in transmigration, with its perpetual succession of rebirths into conditions of woeful individual life unless the soul's unhappy agitations and unrest should be composed by virtue, shapes the moral task mainly, not only into restraint of the appetites and passions, but into such austerity and stern self-abnegation as may prepare the soul, on the death of the body, to attain the perfect repose of Nirvana, the complete extinction of human passions, or, as Buddhism represents, annihilation of conscious individuality in reabsorption into the absolute existence. In this system the aim of morality is not "the right," but the desired good of tranquil happiness, or the final goal of merging self-conscious personality back again into the Great All from which it arose. The ground of the moral striving—it can hardly be called obligation—is the adaptedness of it to secure this result.

Persian Teaching

4. Zoroastrianism (Mazdæism), from about B. C. 1500–1000, confessedly presents an ethical teaching that, among oriental views, is second only to that of the Hebrews. Its theological dualism, which seems to have encroached upon an earlier purer monotheism, of two eternal principles or powers, Ormuzed (Ahura Mazda) the good power, and Ahriman (Angra Mainyou) the evil power, manifestly arose from the effort to solve the dread

problem of evil in the world. Zoroastrian teaching represents Ormuzed as the all-knowing and the holy creator of the world. He cannot create evil. He is the source of all purity, order and righteousness. Wrong and misery have come into the world from Ahriman, the opposite contending power in the universe. Zoroastrianism thus gives the world-system a moral foundation and law of order. The moral life is a holy conflict with the forces of evil within human nature and assailing it. The supreme end of life is to increase the ascendency of righteousness and establish its everlasting reign of truth and goodness. The goal of it comes in a future life of blessedness. The ground of righteousness is thus placed in the nature and will of the eternal creator, to whom obedience is due, against the influences of the malign power of evil.

Greek Theories

5. Among the Greeks ethical philosophy began with Socrates. Their earlier writers dealt with the subject of duty but little in a speculative way. When the philosophy of it came to be sought the theories mainly connected it closely with "the good" or "the highest good," the *summum bonum* of life. This designation was ambiguous. "The good" (τὸ ἀγαθόν, τὰ ἀγαθά) might be conceived of as either intellectual or sensuous good, as consisting in one's intrinsic state or in outward condition, as either happiness or personal well-being. And because this method failed to distinguish clearly and fully between this indefinite "good"—having at best no more authority than "the beautiful"—and "the right" which forms the true essence of the ethical principle, their explanations failed to become clear, and stopped short of being actual explanations of the ground of right. Hence their theories, though not always consistently exhibited, and variously interpreted by expounders of them, were substantially *eudæmonistic* and *utilitarian.* Specifically:

(1) Socrates made all virtue consist in knowledge, especially self-knowledge or wisdom, leading men to proper self-regulation and happiness. He put emphasis upon man's rational nature as essentially good, and to this rational nature belonged the office of

self-mastery and control of all appetites, dispositions, and passions. The life in knowledge became the good and happy life. Though this great sage maintained that the world is governed by a supreme intelligence, he failed to connect clearly and closely the moral law with this high source, and rested the moral life simply subjectively.

(2) Plato developed his view substantially on the basis of that of Socrates. He identified the highest good with the intellect rather than the sensibility, and looked upon all virtues as united in *knowledge*, not only as guiding the soul in acting out its proper destination, but, according to some statements, even as in itself all-sufficing. Though Plato's speculative view of the universe contains the elements for the construction of a sublime immutable ethical standard, and he even suggests God-likeness as the goal of man's moral life, the implications of his view are not consistently carried out; and when he comes to apply his ideas to life in his ideal Republic he lapses into what seems a caricature of his better thought, and is content to rest morality simply on the authority and laws of the state.

(3) Aristotle, in whom Plato's theistic view of the world receded into the background, made the "chief good" consist in happiness or felt well-being, which depends on man's living according to his rational nature. Such living includes both the activities of the mind and habitual conduct. The reason must not only develop its own energies, but rule the lower powers and passions. On this double requirement he founded two kinds of virtue, the intellectual (dianoetic) and the practical. The one consists in "knowledge" or "wisdom," the other in formed "habits" or "character." The moral life, therefore, consists in the true use, without abuse, of our rational nature. The rule for it, as taught by Aristotle, is to avoid extremes and pursue the golden mean. The theory thus rests morality wholly on subjective good and identifies it with the calculations of prudence. It is simply secularistic, without religious element or appeal.

(4) In Epicurus (B. C. 341–270) and his followers eudæmonism descended into hedonism. The supreme good is happiness in the sense of personal enjoyment, pleasure. The universe, without theistic ground, was regarded as eternal, forever evolving in

fortuitous concourse of atoms. It is without rational order, design, or government. The human soul is material, and at death men cease to be. The good of life consists in the avoidance of pain and the securing of pleasure. The pleasure may be intellectual or sensuous and gross, as men may prefer. The pursuit of it is the highest virtue and best wisdom. Enjoyment is the end of life. The whole question of ethics thus came to be a calculation and balancing of pains and pleasures, and the cardinal virtue prudent selfishness. It was complete subjectivism.

(5) In Stoicism (founded by Zeno of Citium, about 308 B. C.) we have a view that, in its principal features, was in strong contrast with Epicureanism. It arose in close relation to the teaching of Socrates. But it taught that "happiness" was not necessary, and should never be made the end of endeavor. Virtue itself was the highest good, and to be sought for its own sake. Itself was sufficient for happiness—not because it could make men insensible to pain or pleasure, but because it made them superior to it. Virtue was immutably excellent in itself, a permanent reality for man's realization, and subordinated everything else. It consisted essentially in living "according to nature," *i. e.* not simply in harmony with one's self, but with the nature of the universe, with the whole constitution of the world as ordained and ruled by God, of which a man's own nature forms a part. The stress was not at all to be laid on self, but upon the great total of being. Man exists for society, and virtue is impossible apart from the social state. So Stoic teaching inculcated subordination of self to more general interests—to family, country, mankind. It taught that all creatures are "children of one father," and duty was owed to all. We may hardly, however, speak of this as "altruism," in the sense of unselfish benevolence or self-sacrificing goodness; since, in the general Stoic philosophy, not the sentiment of sympathetic helpfulness, but of victorious superiority to pain, was the temper fostered. Love was almost submerged in the stern spirit of duty. The blessedness of virtue was to stand independent of the sufferings which befell men. In fact the dreadful inexorableness of fate (εἵμαρμένη), conceived by the Stoic philosophy as eternally embracing the life of both God and nature, gave to virtue, not so

107

much the temper of free, loving obedience to either God or righteousness, as the sternness of a proud intellectual resoluteness in yielding, for virtue's sake, to the inevitable in the fate-bound universe. Under this conception the Stoic moral obedience could never rise to the free joyousness that belongs to the obedient life under the light of the Christian truth that God is love—eternal love, ruling in absolute freedom and desiring to exalt His children to the perfect holiness to which alone happiness forever belongs.

All these Greek theories, except the Stoic, are thus seen to have been marked by two features. First, they dissolved "the right," which alone has direct authority and forms moral law, into "the good," which is simply something offered to us as an object of desire, but which has no "imperative" for the conscience, and may be innocently foregone. Secondly, despite the clear better implications supplied to them in their accepted theistic conceptions of the world, they failed to define distinctly any grounding of the moral law on anything higher or more permanent than the subjective elements of the human constitution. For, even Plato's objective basing of it, for citizen duty, on the law of the state, assumed only a subjective basis in the person of the ruler himself. The Stoic theory, however, had glimpses of some higher and broader ground, though it failed to see it truly.

Roman Teaching

6. The Roman moralists adopted substantially the doctrine of the Greek Stoics. This was finely exhibited and commended, especially by Seneca, Epictetus and Marcus Aurelius. But we have no new theory among the Roman philosophers.

After the establishment of Christianity, whose progress thenceforward determined and marked the intellectual activity and advancing philosophy and culture of mankind, the discussion of ethics became simply a part of theology. And according to the spirit and method of theology in the early Church and during the middle ages, even down to modern times, the discussion was not philosophical, but biblical. It was concerned simply to set forth human duty, especially the duties of the Christian life, as taught in the scriptures of the Old and New Testaments. Resting the moral law upon revealed divine authority, it paid small attention to the question of its metaphysical validation. But when modern philosophy began its investigations, it of necessity soon came upon this point, and inquired after the natural basis or ultimate ground of the great law whose unique authority both the sacred Scriptures and the moral consciousness of men agreed in asserting.

Divine Absolutism

7. Modern theories begin with that of Divine absolutism—making the moral law, like physical laws, only a product of God's will. It makes it rest absolutely optional in His sovereignty of choice. It not only seeks no ulterior reason, or logical *prius*, for his choice, but distinctly disconnects it from any. God's will is not the expression or revelation, but the originator, of the moral distinction, constituting it, with its obligatoriness, as He has done, when He might have constituted it otherwise, even the very contrary. He determined "the right" according to no norm, but as creating and establishing a norm. Whether there should be any moral distinction and what it should be, was a matter of the divine choice. The view is a one-sided conception of God's sovereignty. It was set forth by Hugo Grotius (1583–1645) and Rene Descartes (1596–1650), and has found prominent advocacy frequently since. But it collides with both sound theology and an adequate moral philosophy.

(1) It fails to recognize any eternal essential moral character in God Himself. The interests of both morality and religion require faith in Him as Himself eternally the righteous and holy creator and moral ruler, in His immutable nature. The morally good cannot be something "contingent," but must be absolute, irrepealable and irreversible even by God. We need for both religion and character, to hold fast to the great truth which represents God in His moral will as choosing righteousness as righteousness, loving the "morally good as good"—not as by mere will originating the moral distinction and fixing a code of conduct

upon arbitrary ordination. For real moral character in God we must go even further and regard Him as loving righteousness, not simply as good in Himself, but as good in itself, good by the immutable quality of its own nature. For a moral government we must have a moral governor. And God can be such, not by enforcing responsibility to an arbitrary code, but by ruling according to distinctions that are *per se* supreme in eternal reason—enforcing not a mere rule of power but of essential rightness.

(2) Further, the action of the conscience itself, in discerning right and wrong where it has received no information as to the will of God, implies that the distinction is rationally based. To discern it is not always conditioned on such information. Reason itself—the human in the image of the divine—in some degree reveals the right. So clear is this discernment, and so independent of all "contingency" does the right appear, that even pagan writers have been wont to make virtue superior even to the displeasure of the gods, nobly standing self-approved.

(3) The true relation between the will of God and the ethically good must be conceived of as, indeed, involving a profound and indissoluble identity—what He wills being always and necessarily right, though He wills it in perfect freedom—but yet as moving in the logical order of thought, that right is not made right by His willing it, but that He wills it because it is right.

Civil Authority

8. Thomas Hobbes (1588–1679), holding the natural state of man as utterly selfish and a state of war, gave to civil government, as necessary to the social order, supreme authority, and asserted that the basis of all moral obligation was positive law issued by the sovereign. Duty rested on the legal statute, whose direction was final. It knew no higher law. The theory was a repetition of the travesty of ethics in Plato's Republic. It has had no following, and needs no confutation.

But a theory that thus ignored individual conscience and essential right, reducing morality to civic obedience, with no other foundation than the positive enactment of a monarch, at once and strongly reacted in strengthening the conviction of the necessity and truth of the intuitional view of the moral faculty, and of the importance of finding a better basis for the ethical principle, both in the constitution of mankind and in the author of nature.

The Sympathetic Theory

9. The Sympathetic Theory is naturally associated with that conception of conscience which makes it consist fundamentally, not in intellect, but in instinct or feeling. Taking the suggestion from Hume, the theory was elaborated by Adam Smith (1723–1790). It explained moral obligation as produced by the special action of our nature in which we spontaneously sympathize with certain intentions or conduct of our fellow-men—this sympathy taking the form of approval. The bond to duty was viewed as thus formed by these instinctive sentiments pointing out what is morally good and obligating to corresponding behavior. Of course the individual's sympathetic appreciation had to be broadened and trained by the standard of general sentiment. And the explanation, was helped out by noting the adaptation of this rule of conduct to promote personal and social happiness. But a theory resting duty on a basis so thoroughly subjective, and so uncertain and changeful as are men's unguided feelings, likely often to be in sympathy with evil, could not commend itself to wide acceptance. It presented neither the ground of right nor a safe rule.

Utilitarianism

10. The theory of Utilitarianism had its prototypes in the teachings of Socrates, Aristotle, and the Epicureans. Its modern forms have been greatly varied, but they all agree in founding the morally good in utility. That which experience shows to be useful, as promotive of personal or social interests and happiness, becomes thereby right, or the norm of moral choices and conduct. The theory, in all its modifications, is a "goods" theory, interpreting obligation as simply the behest to conform life to the

attainment of the various forms of good, even the chief, as happiness or enjoyment, provided for in man's nature and condition. Named from the object or objects sought, it is eudæmonism; named from the way or means of its attainment, it is utilitarianism. Sometimes the good is simply happiness, sometimes personal well-being, sometimes social welfare. Sometimes it is purely selfish, sometimes altruistic or in some sense benevolent. But a few examples will make plain both its general character and chief variations.

(1) William Paley (1743–1805), adopting eudæmonistic principles, rested all obligation to duty on its tendency to secure everlasting happiness. He says: "Actions are to be estimated by their tendency. Whatever is expedient is right. It is the utility of any moral rule alone, which constitutes the obligation to it." "The will of God" is accepted as "the rule of virtue," seemingly not, however, as the direct ground of it, but rather as the sure guide as to what has the "tendency" to gain for us "everlasting happiness." For, Paley explains: "Such is the divine character that what promotes the general happiness is required by the will of God." This view makes the spirit of duty, even in religion, supreme selfishness. It places the self-regarding impulses on the throne.

(2) Jeremy Bentham (1748–1832), the chief apostle of modern utilitarianism, gave it great popularity by making it distinctly altruistic. Adopting suggestions in this direction by Shaftsbury (1713), Hutcheson, Butler, and Hume, he measurably lifted its aim above the individual's care of his own interests, and made the principle of right authoritative because promotive of "the greatest happiness of the greatest number." This seemed to subordinate, without excluding, the individual's advantage to that of the many, and the selfish instinct to the higher and nobler aims of love. It developed a rule by which the brotherhood of man could have place, and character could rise and broaden into magnanimity and worth. It gave an objective standing and broadly human aim to the principle of obligation. James Mill, J. S. Mill and Alexander Bain have been conspicuous recent representatives of this general view, while modifying some particular features of it.

It must be added, however, that this modern "altruism," when analyzed to its final view, does not become "disinterested benevolence." For the greatest general good is viewed as conditioning the best good of each individual, and the individual is to include it for the sake of his own share. So this so-called "altruism," after all, is still ruled by the self-regarding aim, and stands only for the broadest and most successful utilitarianism.

(3) Evolutionist Utilitarianism. This is its recent and present most characteristic form. The variety of types of evolutionism, however, has prevented the bringing of it, thus far, into a definite universally accepted formulation. Although, as already stated, monistic evolutionism, whether materialistic or pantheistic, by excluding freedom from the universe, leaves no place for moral action or responsibility, it still continues to speak about obligation and the reality of personal character. In this case the "obligation" can be only acquiescence in the fatalistic onward evolution of nature with its inevitable events. Theistic evolution, however, holding itself as only the mode of the divine creation, though it has difficulties in explaining the genesis of an authoritative conscience, maintains both its existence in some sense and a ground for the obligation which it urges. Its utilitarianism differs from earlier forms in substituting an historical and biological explanation of the origin and force of the moral sentiments for the purely psychological one. These sentiments are declared to be "the results of accumulated experiences of utility, gradually organized and inherited."[2] In its better forms of statement this process of organizing a guiding instinct or intuition is represented as the divine work of transferring the moral law over us into our subjective consciousness—a process, however, that moves on the principle of utility and is always incomplete.

Against the whole utilitarian theory, as a widely urged explanation of the ground of right and the sense of obligation, the following considerations are decisive:

First, the idea of right is generically distinct and different from that of happiness or utility. However closely related they refuse to be identified and must not be confounded. In reference to any particular act or to any general course of conduct, beyond the question of pleasure or advantage arises the further question: Is it right? Every day of their lives men are required to forego enjoyment and the forwarding of what appears to be their interests, in order to do right and follow their conscience. Perceived adaptations to happiness are not the same as the obligation to right. Utilitarianism stands apart from the moral idea, in a by-play with the idea of profit.

Secondly, as a matter of fact, clear in our consciousness, we do not, in deciding the right or wrong of purposes and conduct, go through the process of first determining the question of utility or adaptedness to secure the greatest happiness to the greatest number or even our own greatest happiness. In actual moral experience, the first fact is the notion of right and duty. Even when pleasure or advantage is making an appeal, duty is decided by the further question: Is it right? If it be claimed that the process of calculation has become largely unnecessary through the experience which has been teaching lessons and training into judgments so spontaneous as to seem almost intuitive, there are still cases enough where the right is a distinct issue, irrespective of advantage, and where it is chosen in the face of loss and suffering. This fact shows that right is a distinct principle and higher than pleasure. To do right rather than seek sensitive good is the noblest exaltation of character.

It is especially in evolutionist utilitarianism that the absence of such conscious calculating of advantage in questions of duty, is supposed to be explained. The enjoyment of the useful is represented as gradually organized and transformed into moral approbation, and through hereditary descent appears, as Herbert Spencer says, in "certain emotions responding to right and wrong, which have no apparent basis in the individual experiences of utility." But philosophy fails to explain how the idea of the useful can thus become identical with the idea of the right, or even explanatory of it. If a lifetime's experience of utility does not suffice to transmute the idea of one into the other, why should we think a longer time would do it? If duty does not become the same as happiness or as the tendency of conduct to promote it, in the ascending steps of individual evolution, what warrant have we to assume that it did so in some period far back of the consciousness of the present individuals of the race?

Thirdly, utilitarianism is inconsistent with the authority which belongs to right, as witnessed in the moral consciousness. It is the distinctive peculiarity of conscience that it reveals a law or principle of obligation, not of our own making, and which our wills cannot displace. Manifestly this authority is not of the faculty itself, but belongs to the law of right which it discloses. It is right, therefore, that is authoritative, with and through the conscience, because right is a revelation of that absolute authority not ourselves which makes for righteousness in the world and the whole universe. It represents the perfections and will of God. No theory of obligation is adequate which does not square with this fact of unique authority in right, as recognized and enforced by the moral imperative. But neither happiness nor the utilities that tend to promote it, possess it. They are not obligatory in the peculiar sense in which the ethical behest binds to righteousness. They are offered to our enjoyment, as sensitive good, but we may forego them or neglect to seek them, without direct criminality. Duty may, and often does, require us not to make them a controlling object of desire.

Among pleasures, some are higher or larger than others, and appeal to some persons more strongly than to others. We can innocently choose between them. To seek the greater instead of the smaller, or indeed to neglect them all, is a prudential characteristic, not a moral one. Where a person has simply foregone pleasure, he may regret it as an error, but not repent of it as a sin. Considered with respect to the individual alone, and free from relations that may incidentally involve other points than his own personal pleasure, a man's happiness may be regarded as his own free concern. If he chooses to neglect its pursuit, or sacrifice it to other aims, so far as it is only and purely a question as between greater or less enjoyment, his choice cannot be challenged as guilty, but only as poor economy. Unquestionably it ought to be believed that God desires men to be happy, and has provided the needful conditions for happiness, but its enjoyment is an offer of His love, and not a requirement of law. Happiness is a thing to be gratefully appreciated; right is a thing we are bound to. Happiness is a thing the less likely to be enjoyed the more covetously it is sought after; right claims our unforgetful and completest loyalty. Utilitarianism, therefore, assuming to ground right, which has direct authority in the moral consciousness, upon happiness which in itself has none, necessarily falls short of being an adequate theory of the ethical reality. It attempts to deduce the moral from the non-moral.

This difference between questions of right and questions of utility easily solves a supposed difficulty in the moral freedom of the will. If choices were simply between greater or less degrees of pleasure or advantage, it might easily be imagined that the will would be necessarily determined by the greater pleasure. As between inducements of the same kind, the larger would prevail. But the ethical choices have their place in the presence of motives of different *kinds*, between right and enjoyment, duty or gain; and here there is unquestionable room for free ethical choices. The question of freedom in moral life is at once relieved by taking it out of the utilitarian view into the clear atmosphere where the profitable is no longer confounded with the right.

Fourthly, utilitarianism inverts the true relation between right and utility. Unquestionably the connection between them is very close. In a moral system true happiness belongs to righteousness. Man cannot attain his true welfare in sin. Whatever uncertainties and inequalities the abuse of free agency may bring temporarily into human enjoyment, in the long run right in its very nature promotes the happiness which has been intended for us. But the logical order of relations is, not that an act is right because it is useful, but useful because right. Under a moral government happiness, in the highest and fullest sense, comes as the legitimate fruit of righteousness, as wrong-doing, also, brings its true consequences in suffering, pain and misery. Right is the quality of highest rank, and all blessedness comes into unity and harmony under it. Their rightness gives to actions their quality of usefulness, which cannot, therefore, ground the right. Utilitarianism inverts the real relation.

This true relation explains how it is that the right stands the very highest in the grade of values, without its becoming right by its profitableness. It is of supreme worth, the greatest good, but it is so by what it is in itself. Its good consequences spring from its nature.

But while utilitarianism is thus utterly inadequate as a statement of the ground of right, it nevertheless, especially in its altruistic form, brings to view some genuine and profound principles of the philosophy of duty. This has given it its plausibility and wide acceptance. It is proper, therefore, to mark and recognize the truth that belongs to the theory.

(1) The tendencies of conduct to promote true happiness, or the contrary, furnish, in fact, a valuable practical rule in questions of right and duty. For, by the moral constitution of the world, right-doing, despite the disorders that temporarily obstruct and confuse the real law of consequences, is the way of true welfare. Happiness, in the true, though not hedonistic sense, is an end of our being, and virtue is conducive to it. "The way of the transgressor is hard," under the law of natural cause and effect. The utilitarian theory therefore justly appeals to the great lessons of experienced utility to show the way of duty and guide conduct into righteousness. So that while utility does not explain why an act is right, it becomes, if correctly interpreted, a principle of great value in determining the right.

(2) It is unquestionably true that the altruistic principle of "the greatest good to the greatest number" presents a principle of genuine moral authority. It opens to view the whole realm of obligation to beneficent activity and self-sacrifice. It points to deeds: that are noblest in life and highest in ethical character. It even gives a reason for their obligatoriness. In this form the theory no longer bases duty simply on one's own personal enjoyment or advantage, identifying morality with supreme selfishness, but lifts it into the sphere of benevolence and doing good. For, in altruism individual enjoyment and interests are necessarily subordinated to the well-being of the many. And when utility is thus put into the service of love or good-will, it carries the quality of right into wide ranges of purpose and conduct. It will be observed, however, that the theory thus obtains its appearance of explaining the foundation of right and duty only after "utility" has been itself changed and identified with the virtue of active good-will or beneficence which, of course, is right and obligatory to the degree of every man's ability. In other words, only when it ceases to be purely and

117

really a utilitarian theory, and stands in the name and rights of benevolence—getting ethical authority surreptitiously from the quality of love instead of "profitableness"—does it also get the plausibility that it seems to possess.

(3) It is true, too, that a person's opportunities to promote his own happiness and true interests involve a degree of obligation to do so, as far as this may be consistent with other duties. A proper self-regard is right. In general, on the one hand, we may justly make, as we have done, a distinction between enjoyment, which is offered to our option, and right, which is required by moral law. Were there no considerations involved but that of one's own happiness, this distinction would be unqualified. On the other hand, it must, at the same time, be confessed that the moral consciousness of mankind often condemns the conduct of men reckless of their own happiness or well-being, not simply as "poor economy," but also as morally wrong. Except in benevolent sacrifice no man can innocently throw away his own happiness. The explanation of this is easy. There are other considerations involved than his own happiness. To understand the whole truth at this point the underlying fact must be borne in mind, that man is created for two great ends, primarily for excellence of character, secondarily and consequently for happiness. In moral order the way to the latter is in and through the former. Character stands as the irrepealable condition of reaching man's proper and true happiness. And it is, therefore, true that in throwing away his happiness a man may be guilty of more than "poor economy," but only in case he does this by violating the law of right in surrendering his nature to vice. It is not the consent to surrender enjoyment in itself that involves guilt. For, one may innocently and virtuously forego this for the sake of doing right. He may sacrifice pleasure or present happiness to serve the good of others. In such disregard and sacrifice of enjoyment to do good, there is no, sin against the law of right; for we are not bound to enjoyment as we are to right. Nor is there in it any sin against the divine provision for happiness in our own nature; for under the rule of moral order righteousness and happiness must finally coincide. While, therefore, there is a sense in which to throw away one's happiness is morally wrong, as

well as bad policy, it is only when it is thrown away by conduct that is first a violation of the law of right.

There are two other profound ethical facts which help to explain how men are bound to regard their own happiness, although right is not grounded in it. One is, that every man sustains relations to the welfare of his fellow-men, being a unit in the solidarity of social humanity, making it impossible to separate his own happiness from the well-being and rights of others. The other is that he sustains also relations to an intended possible personal destiny. In the first of these he is bound in duty to his fellow-men. In the second he is obligated in duty to God. In the former case, he cannot wantonly trifle with his own interests without wrong and injury to those to whom he is bound in the relationships of life. In this way a moral wrong comes in. In the latter case, as God has rights in His plan for each man's worthy and happy destiny, it is a sin against Him when men make their own welfare inferior by failure to observe the moral principle which conditions true happiness in righteousness. Sacrifice of happiness by such disregard of moral principle is not to be confounded with sacrifice of it through loyalty to right and holy self-denial in doing good.

It thus, however, becomes evident, even in this discussion and exhibition of the truth which utilitarianism has in its favor, that the theory fails to present the real ground of right. For in its primary and fundamental form, viewing conduct as right because promotive of our personal interests and happiness, it plainly resolves morality into mere calculation of selfishness. It presents supreme egoism. And in its altruistic form it either maintains its selfish character, by explaining that only by the rule of "the greatest good to the greatest number" can the common interest, and consequently each man's share be fully secured, implying that he is to contribute to the common welfare for the sake of his own larger portion; or by subordinating the idea of "utility" to that of "good-will" actively seeking the interests of others, it practically confesses that it must seek some other ground than mere utility or the consequences of conduct, in which to find the principle of right. And this good-will, benevolence or love, thus added, also fails. For since good-will is a virtue, it cannot be placed as the ground of virtue, both in itself and in all virtues. The moral law is by no means exhausted in benevolence; it must include also justice, purity, veracity and many other duties. A benevolence that would be unaccompanied by condemnation of the evildoer and his wrongs, might quickly go astray. It has often been pointed out that good-will itself throws no light as to the right methods of realizing even itself. Itself needs a guide as to how it may proceed—the very principle of right after whose basis we are inquiring. Love, unless united with reprobation of evil-doing, is as likely to act immorally as morally. Benevolent endeavor, however excellent in itself, must subject its methods to the fundamental principles of right. And not until we find the relations that require both benevolence and its utilities, do we reach the ground of right and obligation.

Theory of Relations

11. The Theory of *Relations* is variously modified. As expressed by Dr. Samuel Clarke, right is based on "the fitness of things." Wollaston grounded it on "the truth of things," wrong action being in all cases out of harmony with the realities of existence. Jouffroy found it in the demands of "universal order," the particular good and duty of each man being elements or parts of an absolute good and universal order appearing to reason as obligatory. Dr. Wayland makes right rest upon "conformity of action to the relations which man sustains in life."

We shall come upon the essential features of this theory in our next chapter, in our positive account of the development and basis of right.

Spiritual Excellence Theory

12. As defined by Dr. Hickok: "The ground in which the ultimate rule of right is seen, is the intrinsic excellency of spiritual being." ... "Every man has consciously the bond upon him to do that and that only which is due to his spiritual excellency." But it is a plain matter of fact that men do not go through a process of correlating their proposed conduct with the

spiritual excellency of their nature, before deciding on its moral character. And even if they did so, it would give them but a self-centered rule. Dr. Gregory well says of this attempt to put one's own spiritual excellency as the principle of right: "It is only by a self-deification, by making man a god to himself, that it can be made a supreme end."

Theory of Intuitions

13. Some writers search for no ground beyond the immediate intuition. This view forbears to seek for any basis behind the immediate affirmation of the moral sense. Right is ultimate in its own intuition. "The intuition creates law." This seems to be the teaching of Cudworth, Kant, Coleridge, Calderwood, and others.

Theoretical Ethics

CHAPTER IX

THE GROUND OF RIGHT—CONTINUED

The review of theories in the last chapter prepares us to apprehend the real ground of right. All the subjective theories fail, because the moral quality is objectively real to the percipient conscience. The eudæmonistic and utilitarian explanations are at fault, because they attempt to deduce the moral from the unmoral and can give no account of the unique authority which is the characteristic mark of moral law.

The full ground of right, as the essential elements of the problem have made clearly apparent, must be regarded as twofold, embracing, first, the proximate or immediate ground, and secondly, the ultimate ground.

Proximate Ground Stated

I. The proximate ground—as becomes easily manifest if we keep our view close to the witness of consciousness in actual experience—is in a rational conformity of conduct to the relations which men sustain to one another and to other beings in the divinely constituted system of the world. These relations immediately call for fitting conduct. They create the *ought* of moral law. The right is found in conforming to the requirements which they develop and impose. Duty consists in fulfilling the demands which they involve and express to the moral reason.

This, it will be noticed, accords with the fundamental principle already referred to, that the conception of moral law allies itself normally only with the theistic view of the world, and the truth that the constituted human relations have been framed under a rational ideal of order and welfare. These relations form a rational system in which intelligent free activity is to actualize a divine plan of excellence and well-being. They require conduct in accordance with themselves and with the ends of well-being and happiness to which they have been adapted. The human reason reads the meaning of the relations, and the moral discernment recognizes the obligation to correspondent sentiment and action. Moral conduct thus becomes simply the conduct that actualizes the ideas of divine order to which the framework of human relations has been constituted. What is right springs immediately from the relations, as what is due in ideal moral order. The relations themselves exhibit a moral constitution as the immediate environment of the human moral personality. They bring the ethical requirement which they contain to the recognizing capacity of the reason and the obedience of the will.

It is to be noticed, further, that the term "relations" is to be understood here in its most comprehensive sense and applicability. It embraces all relations with respect to which the human personality in its freedom has to determine and harmonize itself—relations individual, social, and divine. Social relationship has often been absurdly mistaken as the only sphere of moral obligation; and the individual, if contemplated as alone and perfectly isolated, has sometimes been supposed to be entirely without ethical bonds. In what concerns himself only, he is imagined to be unbound. But this is an unwarrantable limitation of the term. For the individual, even viewed utterly apart from his race, yet sustains relations to the adaptations and intentions in his own nature. As in society he owes something to the humanity around him, even alone he would still owe something to the humanity committed to his own keeping. He cannot absolve himself from the bond that binds him to that—as in fact he cannot from that which unites him to his fellow-men. Mere pleasures or enjoyments which are apart from his essential character he may, indeed, disregard, but not what concerns its intended excellence and honor. It has been well said: "Robinson Crusoe did not become a non-moral being when thrown on the desert island; for he still owed respect to his own humanity."

Many a deed is wrong, not as injuring others, but as violative of the agent's relation to the purposes lodged in his own constitution. This is as real as are those that connect him with his fellow-men around him or with God above him. And it is very superficial thought that finds no relations but those that are objective. Sometimes, strangely, in popular thinking, man's relation to God is also omitted from a place in morality, by a relegation of it to the sphere of religion. But this relation is the most fundamental and vital of all human relations and most replete with moral obligations and responsibilities.

This view of the immediate ground of right is fully established by the following additional considerations:

Sustained by Moral Consciousness

1. It is directly sustained by the moral consciousness itself, in constant experience. As a question of psychological metaphysics the point must be settled in harmony with the testimony of consciousness. Appealing to this, there can be no doubt that these relations do develop and call for the duties which the conscience is constantly discerning and enforcing. This is simply a fact—a fact which speculations about the origin of conscience or the education of its judgments, must not be allowed to obscure. It assures that actual morality is no abstraction, but concrete conduct rightly answering to each person's relations in real life. Beyond all question, as thus witnessed in the universal moral consciousness, these relations from the most general, that of man to man, down through all special connections, as between parents and children, husband and wife, brothers and sisters, friends and neighbors, rulers and citizens, employer and employee, rich and poor, capable and helpless, and all the other human interrelations in their thousands of diversified forms, do determine and impose both general and specific duties. The duties come into view as developed by the relations, and change as they are modified and changed. This basing of what is right and obligatory for men on their relations to one another, to God, and to appointed ends, is not a mere theory, but an unquestionable reality in their consciousness.

125

And this accords with the best cosmic philosophy. For this holds all these relations as parts of a rationally designed system of world-order for universal well-being, and the moral reason as capacitated to discern, with more or less clearness and fulness, the moral requirement which they involve and present for observance. We know of no morality that exists, or can exist, in human life, apart from them. Strike them all away, and all duties disappear. Take, as illustration, the most generic virtue of all the virtues recognized by the ethical judgments, that of good-will or love. The moral reason recognizes this as resting, according to eternal fitness, in the broadest and most generic of all relations, that of one intelligent sentient being to another. In the inter-human connection it is based in the brotherhood of man. And this generic good-will, thus required in ideal moral right by the generic relation, becomes differentiated and modified in thousands of special types and forms by the endlessly diversified particular relations of life.

Presuppositions in Responsibility

2. It is implied in the logical presuppositions to all moral responsibility. Among such presuppositions, as conceded by all, are intelligence to know, and freedom to conform to these relations. These prerequisites are essential to the very conception of moral action and amenability. It is the universal sense of the race that creatures that cannot know themselves and the relations they sustain, and are without free-will to fulfil them, are morally irresponsible and incapable of virtue or vice. To them the moral realm becomes a blank, and the moral judgments become impossible. And equally universal is the admission that the moral insight is helped and responsibility increased by every increase of light giving larger and truer knowledge of the complex and intricate connections of human life. With every broadened and clarified vision of these connections fresh obligations appear. "A defective apprehension of the relations in which we stand to God and to our fellow-men, will prevent our seeing our specific duties." This fact furnishes direct evidence that right conduct

must be held as a certain intelligent adjustment to the relations sustained.

The value of this point is magnified when we remind ourselves how it explains and illuminates the sometimes troublesome phenomenon of different and even conflicting moral judgments in the same case by different persons, and the fact of progress in moral standards as civilization and culture advance. Differing apprehension of one or more of the many elements or factors converging, with confusing force, into almost every situation which calls for duty, easily accounts for most of the perplexing diversity. The relations are seen from different angles, and interpreted in different light. And the advance of civilizations, with their science and philosophy, brings truer and completer views of man's place and relations. The moral ideas of the human reason are, indeed, essentially identical in all men and all ages, and when human relations are apprehended in the same light, with equal clearness and fullness, the moral judgments substantially agree. But the progress of knowledge, throwing increasing light on these relations, leads the onward civilizations up into truer and better application of the principles of right in life. The different codes do not mean a change of primary moral ideas, but merely reflect and illustrate the changed and advancing apprehension of man's true relations to which these unchanging ideas are, and are forever to be, applied.

Another and kindred fact is explained, adding still further confirmation of the correctness of this theory. With perfect intentions men fulfil objective duty only in measure. Duty is only approximately accomplished, in varying degrees, from very faulty success to high grades of accuracy and completeness. A correct view of the ground of right must necessarily allow a consistent explanation of this fact. Sometimes the fact has been looked upon as inconsistent with any absolute dividing line between right and wrong, on one or the other side of which every action must fall. Not all good acts are perfect or faultless; not all evil ones are equally violations of duty. Of right actions some measure up better than others toward all that full duty requires. Dr. Martineau, partly in order to account for this scope of variety in moral correctness, urges a special definition of right and wrong:

"Every action is right, which, in presence of a lower principle, follows a higher; every action is wrong, which, in presence of a higher principle, follows a lower." By the great difference in the rank of moral motives the reason of men's differing grades in the ascending or descending scale of character seems to come into view. But while the definition furnishes a rule frequently serviceable for guidance in questions of duty, it fails to define the ground of right; for it leaves unsettled the very point in this question, viz.: why one principle (as a motive) *is* morally "higher" or "lower" than another, or why some intentions or actions are right or wrong in any degree. And the offered explanation is unnecessary; for the unquestionable principle of moral requirement developed in relations, and discerned by the intuitive insight of the conscience fully explains the variety, when we remember the various degrees of accuracy and fullness with which these relations are understood and estimated. Every relation calling for duty is composite and complex, the various parts being often so connected as to come only partially or one-sidedly into view, preventing full insight of the moral demand, or accurate adjustment of sentiment and conduct to it. Rarely is any relation simple and alone. Often, indeed commonly, conscience has to decide duty as a resultant obligation out of very complicated and even antagonistic relationships. All this is amply sufficient to explain the different degrees in which the conduct meets duty. It is the necessary result of the impossibility of exactly fitting the moral sentiment or act to the demands of the moral relations. And the transparent explanation which this theory furnishes of the fact of such degrees strongly corroborates its scientific correctness.

Verified in Moral Concepts

3. It is verified, further, in the character of the various virtues, and their opposite immoralities. In their very conceptions these imply relations. They are molded by them, and carry the shaping thus received. Justice, for example, in inter-human affairs, is absolute equity between man and man—exact reciprocity. Veracity expresses something that is due from one to another

among beings whose welfare requires them to live according to the truth of things. The duty to speak the truth answers to the need and right of each one to know it. Love, or good-will, has already been shown to express the feeling which, in eternal fitness, is due from one sentient rational being to another, in the most generic relationship. Honesty means seeking equality of values in dealings one with another. Sincerity signifies genuineness in the temper and way we relate ourselves to those about us. We might run through all the precepts of the Christian Decalogue and note that everyone is based on some general or special relation, either of man to God or of men to their fellowmen. No virtue can get away from relations. The very concept of every one is molded by them, and carries the shaping which they enstamp upon it as the coin does that of the die.

Supported by Analogy

4. It is supported also by the analogy of organic and instinctive action. In organic action, the physically right is adaptation to environment, in which "each part and movement fills its sphere and accomplishes its functions in the given place and relations. In instinctive action, the force is adjusted to the position and connections in which the animal is placed. For example, that of the bee is made to move correspondently to its relations to the individuals of its own kind and to the end of supporting and preserving the species. The instinct of the beaver adjusts its house to its peculiar surroundings; that of birds constructs their nests in distinct adaptation to the conditions that surround them. In animals that harvest and store their food, it suits the action to the particular environment and changing seasons. In every case instinct fits the activity to the given place and relations of its subject. This method by which organic and instinctive functions are set to secure right action in their special spheres, is exceedingly significant of the generic principle of all right action. In the light of the analogy, the morally right is a continuation of the same principle of harmony with constituted relations which is seen to be omnipresent in all the lower domain of nature extending up to human personality, but becoming

moral at this point by being subject to free will and accomplished by it. It is to be remembered that teleologic plan and adaptation run through the entire cosmic order, from atoms to worlds and from minutest structures of body to the loftiest endowments of intelligent beings akin to God. Automatic action secures accordance in the inferior ranges. The grand distinction of the moral realm appears when, as the crowning ascent of life is reached, the principle of ethical harmony with divinely constituted relations is to be accepted and accomplished by the intelligence and freedom of man and is made the moral *ought* under personal responsibility.

Assumed in Common Life

5. It adds confirmation to this explanation, that it is implicitly assumed in all the conceptions and language of common life. Unbiased by speculative theories the every-day thinking and speech of mankind connect duties with men's personal place and relations—duties modified and fixed according to the form and specialty of individual situations. The fact of duty itself is not more certain than this fact of the way in which spontaneous and unperverted thought grounds it. This fixing of the world's conceptions and speech in this form cannot be fairly interpreted as a caprice or accident, but as the true effect of the actual reality, which stands as its cause or warrant. And it is significant that speculative theorists who have framed for themselves some other account, whenever momentarily off their guard or forgetting to act as watch-dog for their theory, have been wont to turn unconsciously into forms of expression recognizing this relational ground for human duties.

The Ultimate Ground

II. In thus finding the right grounded directly on conformity to the relations given men in the constituted order of life, we have not yet reached the full solution of the great problem. For these relations are only a part of the aggregate moral constitution, and are not the last term of moral authority. They do not stand in their own independent right. Though they do directly create and shape the immediate duties for which they call, they are not the ultimate reality in which moral law has its deep foundations. So we must go back to the source and reason of these relations. The ultimate ground can be found only in God himself who, in his underived eternal nature, is the absolute ground of the whole created universe, with all its interrelations which develop the reality of moral law.

The true conception of the divine creative action is that in it the thought and moral character of God become transitive and appear in the relations established and the ethical requirements which the relations impose. The constituted connections and order of life, which involve an ideal standard of right conduct and duty, reveal the divine mind or intention and in it the ultimate authority. The proximate basis, already discovered, in ideal conformity to the moral relations in which the moral agent is placed, therefore represents God, who, as the first cause and eternal ground of the creation with all its adaptations and laws, is the ultimate and unchangeable ground of right and of all moral law.

This statement of the ultimate ground means more than a resting of right simply on the will of God. A reference of it to his will has often stood for a claim that the moral law stands merely in the option of God or as only a product of his choice. Many have represented it as only an effect whose cause is an act of his will—that will originating or making "the right" rather than observing and declaring it, and the moral law having no basis other than such enactment of will. But this would imply that God himself is without moral character, acting from no norm of essential right, but simply by mere will ordaining what should pass as right among mankind. Our fundamental ethical conception of him, however, is that of a moral being and moral ruler. And to be moral means to love and choose the right as right. We must keep in mind here the relation between moral law and will, or the choices of the will. Moral authority does not exist as will, but as right. The great conception of the right, as witnessed to in universal conscience, is of something that appeals to will and requires the will to bow to its claim. Right is superior and authoritative for will, and cannot, therefore, be simply an effect of it. The right itself is basal for right willing, even with God himself. He wills according to it. Hence the moral law is not to be considered a product of his will, but an expression of his nature. In perfect freedom he wills the good because he is good, being in his eternal nature the absolute and infinite moral Perfection. It is a deep conviction in the moral consciousness of mankind, that God himself is in his very nature righteous and good, a conviction which utters itself evermore in the spontaneous exclamation: "Shall not the judge of all the earth do right!" Out of a non-moral ground the moral could never arise, and only in the very nature of God himself as perfect, infinite and unchangeable righteousness, do we reach the ultimate ground both of the constituted relations of human life and of the sublime and inextinguishable reality of moral law for the ordering of these relations. The profound meaning of the poet's couplet:

"For right is right since God is God,
And right the day must win,"

is to identify God and right as united in the eternal foundation of the moral system. There is thus, for the universe, what has been often designated "an eternal and immutable morality" whose authority and standard rest in the very Ground of the universe itself.

The conclusion thus apparent is vindicated by the very conception of the authority which binds men ethically. Mere "might cannot make right" or be that which has the reverence of the moral nature. Moral sovereignty does not attach to a simple absolutism of power. The ethical will bows to the right only. It would be a great contradiction to think of the power to which the moral submission of the soul is due as itself anything other than an ethical power, the morally good power, the morally good Being.

This ultimate ground of right, thus found, makes plain why ethics, in its full meaning and issue, is so closely allied to religion. Religion, in its spirit and aim, means fellowship with God, accordance of desire, will, and life with him. And ethics, even in the view of its early student Plato, looks to the same goal,

132

"likeness to God." The supreme aim of Christianity is ethical, the transformation and exaltation of human conduct and character into the excellence and happiness of righteousness. That the moral life of man may, out of his broken, corrupt and disabled state of sin, thus become again harmonized with God and the divine constitution of things, redemption comes with its supernatural powers and help for human nature, enabling and accomplishing a realization of the ethical law in human character.

Theoretical Ethics

CHAPTER X

THE OBJECTS OF MORAL JUDGMENT

A full view of the ethical reality and its meaning for us requires yet an examination into the question: Of what may we justly affirm moral quality? Where does the conscience apply the distinctions of right and wrong? What are properly the objects, and the only objects, of moral approval or condemnation? Or, to put it in a way possibly more easily understood, to what human activities or features of life does moral quality belong?

It has already been noted in general that only personal beings can be moral agents or become, in what they are and do, objects of moral judgment. Apart from personality, no place for virtue or vice can be found. Of things, whether natural products or products of human industry, as rock or star or stream, or ship or watch or engine, we cannot predicate moral character. We may speak of them as beautiful, useful, or perfect, or as ugly, useless, or faulty, but all distinctly ethical terms are inapplicable to them. The moral approbation or condemnation which we feel for the temper, words, and actions of men is felt toward them as personal phenomena. Detached from personality they would no more be subjects of praise or blame than the temperature of the sea, the noise of the wind, or the down-pour of rain. Moral character belongs to them only as the characteristics and manifestations of the self-conscious and self-directed life of a moral agent. To the question what activities of a moral agent may have ethical quality, it ought to be sufficient to say that it belongs to all his conscious and self-directed conduct. Obligation claims sway over the whole personality. But for clearness and definiteness, it is necessary to specify.

Personal Actions

1. The action itself, in its external form, may be right or wrong, as in conformity to moral relations or incongruous with them. It may be either the deed that is due to the relations and a fulfilment of the duty they call for, or it may be one that clashes with their rational and actual requirement. It may be in itself just the action in which conduct is rightly adjusted to the actual relations—an act that ought to appear in them. Or it may be in itself an action whose very form contradicts the moral demand of the relations, and which ought not to be done, no matter how good a motive may prompt the deed. For example, the motive to use them in a worthy charity could never justify a theft of goods or money, nor could filial care of a helpless parent be in itself wrong, even should a bad motive inspire it. Moral law repudiates the first deed; it condemns the wrong motive in the second, but declares the material of the deed itself to be right and good.

We must here distinguish between the moral character of the doer and of the deed. The quality of right and wrong belongs to the action; guilt or innocence belongs to the person. This is the basis of the well-known fact that in some cases the doer of a wrong act may nevertheless be held as innocent and even virtuous in it. He may have honestly meant to do right, and acted from praiseworthy motives, but from not understanding correctly or fully the situation, may have done what has violated the moral call of the relations. The action may be condemned, while he himself may be acquitted of guilt. The full ethical demand, however, requires such a use of all our faculties of knowledge and behavior, as not only to maintain a good intention, but to keep our outward conduct in harmony with objective righteousness.

Many writers have shown a disposition to deny moral quality to the external action. Locating it all in the inner sentiment or intention, their analysis separates the visible part from its source, and holds up to view the action, so separated, as mere physical motion, characterizable as useful and expedient or the contrary, but neither moral nor immoral. Independently of its motive it is resolved into mere natural movement, as non-ethical as a muscular spasm, sleepwalking, the dashing of a wave, or the biting of frost. But this is as misleading as it is plausible. The error becomes clear by the following considerations:

(1) The supposed separation of the deed from the inward intention falsifies the actual facts in the case. The essential element in the problem is that we are contemplating, not physical movement only, like spasms or waves, but personal deeds, as acts of moral agents. Of course, moral quality does not attach to the action of non-moral beings, as the striking of clocks or the barking of dogs, but to deeds of self-directing personality. Let it be freely admitted that the inner sentiment does give quality to conduct. The obligation to the conduct that shall fulfil duty attaches to the personal agent; the innocence or guilt also belongs to him. But there *is* obligation upon him with respect to conduct only because conduct, in its external forms as well as inward springs, forms the total material of morality. There could be no responsibility for conduct if no moral quality belonged to actions. To separate—after the manner referred to—the action from the personal moral agent and think of it as physical motion only, makes it no longer the action about whose character we are inquiring.

(2) We must bear in mind several just distinctions in the application of the term right. Along with duty, obligation, merit, innocence, or guilt, it may be affirmed of the moral agent. We may say, "he is right," in doing so or so. We may speak of the inner sentiment as right or wrong. So we may of the external action. For the true and full extent of moral quality, we must make it cover the agent himself, and both the inner and outer sides of his personal conduct. Conduct has an internal and an external part. The motive is only one part. An action is relatively right, with respect to the agent, when he has the right will in right motive; it is absolutely right only when it is also shaped into accordance with the relations so as to realize the moral demand upon the person. The distinction, often made, between formal right and material right, throws the point into clear light. It is well stated by Prof. Bowne: "The former depends upon the

attitude of the agent's will toward his ideal of right, the latter depends on the harmony of the act with the laws of reality and its resulting tendency to produce and promote well-being. Conduct which is formally right may be materially wrong; and conduct which is materially right may be formally wrong; but no conduct can be even formally right when the agent does not aim to be materially right. The ideal of conduct demands both formal and material rightness, and as long as either is lacking the outcome is imperfect.... If one does 'the best he knows,' it is often said nothing more can be demanded of him. And yet it is plain that this formal righteousness is altogether insufficient for the person's well-being. The reason is that the law of well-being is independent of our will. If we misconceive that law and act accordingly, we may be formally right, but because of the misconception we should be materially wrong. It is, then, by no means sufficient that one be formally right, that is, true to his convictions of duty; he must also be materially right, that is, in harmony with reality and its laws. Formal rightness, of course, is ethically the more important, as it involves the good will; but material rightness is only less important, as without it our action is out of harmony with the universe."

(3) The moral consciousness, when unperverted by speculative theory, does in fact judge the actions of men. It steadily holds them as essentially right or wrong, over and above all question as to the motives for them. It is found perpetually condemning even well-meant deeds as traversing duty and righteousness, hardly able to excuse the blundering ignorance to which they are due. This feeling of reprobation is genuine, normal, and wholesome. On the other hand the overthrow of this feeling and the adoption of the claim of a non-ethical character for actions, tends directly and strongly to consequences which witness against the validity of the claim. The demoralizing effect has often been illustrated. The resolving of duty into a mere matter of good intentions has led off into ways and forms of behavior shocking to enlightened consciences. It has made quite plausible the illusion that "the end sanctifies the means," and in the name of religion has stretched men on the rack and lighted the faggots at the stake. Under a fancy that purity is simply a

thing of the heart, men have been known to excuse not a little sensualism of life. While ethics must lay stress on the inner good-will, it must also look after the harmony of the outward acts with the law of right relations. No amount of good motive can make blasphemy or murder right or virtuous.

The Feelings, Passions and Desires

2. The various feelings, passions, and desires are not only springs of action that may issue in conduct, but are in themselves either right or wrong, according as they are exercised in harmony with moral law or in conflict with it.

(1) Though our feelings spring spontaneously and immediately out of our knowledge and fundamental psychical character, they are subject to training and regulation by the will, and their states and movements are part of our moral life. And though by natural unperverted constitution all these primary feelings and affections have right and good functions, their activities, under noxious stimulation, may run into forms and in directions thoroughly immoral. Love, which, in its holiest direction, toward God, and in its purest forms of benevolence, toward men, is the highest virtue, may take forbidden directions and corrupt and disorder life. Hate, the reverse of love, instead of being directed against evil which ought to be hated, often emits its venom against that which ought to be loved for its goodness. Self-esteem, as a proper respect for what has been put into a person's being to be cared for and enjoyed, frequently runs into condemnable selfishness. Many of the "desires" are apt to be in offense because of over-development, clashing in anarchic insubordination in the soul, or rushing toward unlawful objects. Desire for possessions tends to grow into covetousness, desire for honor into unscrupulous ambition, desire for pleasure into a ruling passion. Such feelings as malice and envy, mongrel products of selfishness and ill-will, are at once adjudged to be sinful.

(2) Were further proof needed that morality attaches to the affections and desires, it is found in their relations as motives to conduct. We have not traced actions completely to their moral

source when we have ascertained the volition from which they proceed. We must go a step further back and mark the impulses that either rightly or wrongly influenced the will. We must do as do courts of justice in seeking the character of an act, and ascertain not only that the act was done in free-will, but also what feelings influenced the free-will in doing it. An act of volition may have very different motives behind it. The immoral character of the volition is not only from the immorally-acting will itself, but also from the wrong feelings or desires acting on the will. Indeed, the very will is betrayed into wrong-doing by their perverting persuasions. It becomes clear, therefore, that if it be at all true that "actions take moral character from their motives," this character must be predicable of these motive sensibilities.

(3) A special question has place here—whether moral quality belongs even to the personal dispositions, propensities and inclinations that lie back of the *exercise* of the feelings, as attitudes or habitudes of the soul with respect to good and evil? The facts of life unquestionably show the existence of such propensities or tendencies derived through heredity and descending from generation to generation. The scientific theory of evolution recognizes them and draws many of its conclusions, both psychological and moral, from them. They express rather a state of the personal constitution than any exercise of its faculties. They denote so basally the psychical life condition, that they characterize rather what the person is than what he does morally. Since they, as states of the personal agent, constitute his attitude, among other things, toward good and evil, an attitude either right or wrong, this question manifestly requires an affirmative answer.

Aims and Intentions

3. Intentions. In judging conduct we inquire especially into the aim, purpose, intention, which directed it. We look at the end sought. And in a peculiar degree conduct is pronounced right or wrong according to this. For the intention is pre-eminently the very heart and informing principle of the moral act. Besides

largely shaping the material action in agreement or conflict with objective duty it is the inner soul of the total deed.

It may make an act that in its external form is morally indifferent thoroughly virtuous or deeply criminal—such as that of handing a sum of money to another, in one case to relieve suffering, in another to secure murder. The intention to do what is known to be wrong, even when the overt deed is prevented, stamps upon the person its own moral character.

In intentions we find the teleology of the ethical conduct—the chosen ends at which men are aiming in their constant endeavor—and they have a place of importance corresponding to this directive relation. Life moves as these turn, and the great body of human activity, in its mighty sweep of purposive conduct, whether rising into its loftiest and purest virtues or descending to its lowest and most horrid crimes, is their result. In this teleological position they differ as "motives" from the motives found in the simple feelings, affections and passions which act non-voluntarily and unconscious of ends, but are springs of impulse and incentives from the subjective psychical organization. Intentions are deliberate voluntary purposes aiming at chosen objects and adjusting means to ends. For this class of motives, therefore, we are peculiarly and pre-eminently responsible.

Activities of the Intellect

4. The activities and uses of the intellect. Often theorists have denied any moral element in these, mainly because of a certain "necessity" in intellect under psychical law, and because its function is simply "to know." It does nothing, either good or bad; "it only knows." Its sphere is the sphere of knowledge, not of conduct. But this is a very inadequate view of its total activity, and of its place in the moral agent's life. As to the question of "necessity," the activities of the intellect are as much under the command of the moral agent as are his sensibilities, his affections, desires, and passions. It would be difficult to see why he should be amenable for the direction and regulation of these desires and passions, and not also for the direction and character of his

intellectual work and the use he makes of these high endowments. As to the question of the non-moral character of cognitive or thought activities, they are correctly conceded to be, in very large measure, without any ethical quality. But it is also true, that there may be activities, as for example, in the imagination, and in purposive scheming, which are impure and grossly violative of justice and right. Because the intellect in itself, as contradistinguished from the will, does not choose and has no choice, we may not, indeed, say of its activity: "It is guilty," "it is under obligation," since obligation and guilt pertain not to the act but to the moral person; but yet we may speak of intellectual activity or work as morally "right" or "wrong," according as it is in harmony or in conflict with the true ends for which the intellectual powers have been framed and the well-being they are designed to serve. It would be difficult to see why the intellectual activity which plans out the details of a theft or a murder is not as really immoral, *i. e.* something morally condemnable, as is the desire or wish to commit it, or why the person is less blameworthy for the one than the other. In both cases it is part of his personal activity. And if he is "blameworthy," it is only because the activity is in itself "wrong." Is he any less guilty for allowing his intellect to think out the wrong than his feelings to desire it? The moral sense must condemn this intellectual work as inconsistent with the relations of the intellect to human well-being and righteousness. In these days of worship of intellectual brilliancy, and the large prostitution of the imagination to activities which flood literature with thoughts that defile and suggestions that carry moral blight and desolation, producing every form of vice and crime, it is of prime importance to recognize that this intellectualism does not stand altogether apart from moral quality, and that men are under the completest obligation to keep it all in harmony with righteousness and the ethical ends of life.

Acts of the Will

5. Our view of intentions has touched on part of the functions of the *will* with respect to moral quality, but its acts in the stricter

sense and more specific forms require further statement. "Intentions" are, indeed, under the command of the will, yet they are there as motives, whose force and quality stand specially in the objects desired and aimed at. They draw their quality rather from the ends sought than from the working of the will which consents to the ends. We must see yet whether the conscience judges also the proper and specific acts of the will.

Of course that which we name "the will" is simply the soul's power of choosing, or rather, it is the personal self as causal for choices and executive action. Its acts are "volitions." Does moral quality attach to these? There can be no doubt of it. Upon these volitions, preferential and executive choices, electing between duty and its opposite, between conduct in harmony or in conflict with moral requirement, between indulgence of good or wicked feelings, between virtuous and evil intentions, between higher and lower motives, between actions materially right or wrong, making the decision for or against righteousness and goodness and purity, in all the questions of daily behavior in which life rises into ethical excellence and blessedness or descends into wrong, vice, crime, and consequent wretchedness, the moral sense of mankind pours its most unequivocal approvals or reprobations. It not only judges them as right or wrong in themselves, but as, among all human activities, most creative or most destructive of moral character. It is a fundamental postulate in ethical thinking that moral law binds the will.

In the action of the will the moral judgment finds its object of highest approval and of most thorough condemnation. It is to the will, i. e. the personal self, that moral law presents its claims. It is the point in which personality is summed up in free and responsible selfhood, and where the great reality of responsibility is pivoted. The will, as another name for the soul's power of choosing, sustains the decisive relation between all the motives that precede and the actions which follow the volitions. The action contemplated may be right or wrong, the motive may be good or bad, but when the question is brought by the conscience into the presence of the will, the place of supreme and final responsibility for virtue or sin is reached.

This justifies the conclusion that moral character belongs to the exercise of the will as it does not to any other activity of our moral nature. For it is the point, and the only point, of freedom in our whole constitution. Necessity marks the action of each and every part from the lowest functions up to the will; and beyond this there stretches on another realm of necessity in the consequences of volition. For example, necessity rules in the physical nature. The processes go on under fixed uniform laws, with no freedom or choice. So in the intellect and the sensibility. We begin to think in non-optional spontaneity, or we would not think at all. In perception, representation, in the discursive and intuitive powers, and in the emotions, affections and desires that arise from the activity of the intellect, the movement is bound up under laws of cause and effect. Whatever power of regulation, change or control we possess over these functions does not belong to the powers themselves, but to the will or the personal capacity of free choice and self-regulation. It is only through our will-power that we can handle and direct our thinking or control the direction and force of our feelings. So, too, the ideas of right and wrong, the perceptions of duty and the sense of obligation come into the presence of the will of necessity. All before the will is of necessity. Thus men see the right and perceive obligation. At this point all the responsibility of character is thrown upon the will. If contemplated action appear right or wrong, as action that ought or ought not to be done, the will must decide whether it shall be done. If good or bad motives plead for rulership, the will must say which shall prevail. If feelings are out of harmony with duty and right in the relations of life, with respect to God or man, it is to be remembered that the feelings cannot choose, and the will alone can guide them in virtuous action. To it, therefore, virtue or guilt belongs as nowhere else. For it not only accepts and makes its own all the right or wrong that appears elsewhere, but it also remains true or becomes false to its own supreme duty and obligation to moral law, when, under the behests of conscience, it directs life and character either up the heights of moral excellence and happiness, or into the wrong and guilt and miseries of immorality. Where the will is moral the man is moral;

for the will is the zenith of personality. Where it is immoral the man is immoral.

CHAPTER XI

THE ETHICAL VIEW UNDER CHRISTIAN TEACHING

These conclusions with respect to the nature and office of conscience, the ethical distinction, its theistic implications, its transcendental character and objective validity, its relation to personality and freedom, the proximate and ultimate ground of right, and the different parts of human activity to which moral quality belongs, are conclusions reached by the scientific method and stand on the warrant of reason. They arise from phenomena of history and life, and form, in their essential statements, a body of scientific and philosophical knowledge of equal certainty and authority with the most assured results of other branches of rational investigation. Ethics, therefore, finds its fundamental truths in the natural constitution of the world, and is able to build these truths into a science possessed of all the rights and force of systematized and established knowledge.

Christianity Recognizes Ethics

1. Christianity fully recognizes these truths and all the essential principles which ethical science formulates and certifies. It does more. It magnifies their importance by building upon them its own divine view of moral requirement and the way of its realization. All that ethical science shows to be true in the moral constitution of man, in the reality of moral law for the free regulation of his conduct, and in respect to the source and immutable authority of that law, abides as fundamental

147

presuppositions in the divine superstructure of religion and duty presented by Christianity. Redemption starts and works upon the basal facts of human nature and man's condition, relations, duties, responsibilities and needs. If Christianity assumes the existence and rulership of God, a moral constitution of human life, and the existence of conscience with its perceptions of duty and sense of obligation; if it assumes man to be a free agent and yet bound in the exercise of his autonomy by laws of obligation and responsibility; if it assumes the law of right to be essentially unalterable and irrepealable, a reality to which God himself conforms, all these are great truths fully certified in the rational conclusions of ethical science.

Contributions to Ethical View

2. But Christianity contributes immensely to the ethical view. It is, indeed, a great misconception to think that supernatural revelation has been given simply to teach morality, or to look on Christianity as merely a code of ethics. But though its first great object is redemption, presenting God to our view in redeeming love and activity, and offering deliverance from the guilt and life of sin, it necessarily also aims to recover men to personal righteousness. Indeed, both forgiveness and renewal look to this as the goal to which redemption is to bring its subjects. While primarily Christianity is a religion and redemptory, its ultimate aim is the establishment of men in obedience to God, righteousness, and excellence. The very summit of its purpose, the Alp that rises above every other Alp, is character and right life. So the very law of its movement is supremely ethical. Forgiveness of sin, justification by faith, stands as only the first step in the application of redemption, and beyond this Christianity pre-eminently means a life, the increasing recovery and perfection of human nature in its ethical character and action, enthroning the principles of duty, love, and righteousness in the conscience and the heart, and bringing personal conduct into rhythmic harmony with eternal righteousness and goodness.

And the science of ethics has not properly completed its view until it has fully included the distinctive teaching of Christianity.

For beyond all question the data of this teaching have produced the purest and loftiest moral life that the world has seen, the best product of the moral history of mankind. Its ideal is confessedly the highest and the best sustained. Even apart from the question of the well-proved supernatural claims of Christianity, its ethical work lifts its moral teachings to the most authoritative place, the supreme court, for the decisions and formulations of the complete scientific view.

The total contribution of Christianity to morality comes along two lines of help: 1. In the way of fuller disclosure of moral principles and of essential duties; and 2. In the way of furnishing an efficient dynamic for their fulfilment. The first of these two topics claims attention in this chapter; the second must be left for the next.

The need of larger knowledge, than that furnished by simply naturalistic ethics, for the perfection of moral life, has everywhere been evident. The debasement of moral thought and the worse debasement of moral life frequently found among peoples outside of the atmosphere illuminated by Christian truth, is sad proof how crying this need of right knowledge may become. The strife of conflicting opinions as to the root and validity of moral principles, even among many in Christendom who look at the subject with faces averted from Christianity, is perpetual remembrance of the room for more and better information. And the perplexing phenomenon of wide diversity of moral judgments in daily life, to which we have had occasion several times already to refer, resulting from the different degrees of correctness with which the relations of life are understood and interpreted, enforces the same truth. The moral power is educable. It sees its objects in the light, not in darkness, nor fully in dawn. It acts best when flooded with the fullest knowledge. Men can discern duty accurately and fully only when they comprehend all their relations to God above them, their fellow men around them, their destiny before them, and the significance and moral demand of these relations. From the high origin of their nature, "in the image of God." they may carry some impress of the moral law from God in their hearts, in the inner order of insight and spiritual vision, and in measure "read God's thoughts after Him" about love and justice and truth and other essential virtues. But this rational reading of duty from the law of right within them and from the moral constitution about them, is grandly helped when revelation throws its illumination on the nature and relations of men, the meaning of life and the reach of its responsibilities. Whatever has been the short-coming of Christianity's professors in exemplifying its moral teaching, the history of its work is full proof of its containing the best ethical direction and power the earth has yet seen. In individuals and communities in which its teachings have been worthily turned into character and life, it presents an inspiring suggestion of what it is capable of doing for human exaltation when its instruction is truly followed. It is the completing factor for moral guidance, and the scientific view is false to itself when it fails to include the teachings and the phenomena of the Christian consciousness and life. Since Christianity has come and given the world its highest civilizations and elevations, its grandest progress in philosophy, science, art, literature, invention, enterprise and prosperity, all the purest and most beautiful amenities of life, and is still leading the best nations onward and upward, it is surely worse than idle to think of forcing ethical science back to a pagan or merely naturalistic standpoint. This would ignore the greatest moral phenomenon of history and the most impressive facts in the present condition of the world. "Christian ethics is ethics in the highest—ethics raised to the highest power—the last and fullest moral interpretation of the world and its history."

Sources of Christian View

3. The Christian ethical view has its special moral conceptions from two sources. The one is primary and principal; the other secondary and auxiliary.

(1) The principal source is the Sacred Scriptures of the Old and New Testaments. Along with their distinctively religious purpose and teaching, these pages of God's supernatural revelation, from first to last, look to ethical ends, and are replete with principles, laws, and precepts for duty and righteousness. As for a knowledge of Christianity as a religion we must come to

these writings as its own accredited records, presenting its truths and requirements, so also for a knowledge of its moral teachings. Whatever help may be obtainable from other sources, say from study of the Christian consciousness or of the effects of Christianity on personal and social life, the chief and highest source is these Sacred Scriptures. For the best Christian life falls short of the ideal standard of conduct there presented. It would be unfair to study it or judge it only in the partial, fragmentary, one-sided, imperfect illustrations of it. Every ideal thus gained must be corrected and greatly upraised before it can stand for the complete divine ideal that shines out from the teachings of the Scriptures and the life of the Christ therein revealed. The perfect image of Christian ethics has never been fully reflected by either the inward or outward life of the believer The Sacred Scriptures, therefore, are the only infallible normative authority for Christian ethics, as they are for Christian theology.

This use of the Scriptures as the determinative authority, however, must take account of the fact that they present an historical and progressive revelation. As God's redemptive action advanced historically, unfolding religious truth and grace gradually and educationally, so the moral ideal, which Christianity in its fullness of provision and power should exhibit, is found more and more clearly revealed till the view is completed. This accounts for the higher ethical view reached in the New Testament.

The Old Testament, which is the record of the earlier stages of the Christian revelation, distinctly preparatory and prophetic, forms a continual instruction in duty and righteousness. It grounds the moral life essentially in the religious, but religion must walk in holiness. Fundamental in it stands the Decalogue, a summary of moral law, of most profound and comprehensive sweep, which is still the great code of duty for the guidance of human conduct, and so clearly beyond the mere thinking of Moses or the people he led, as to prove its divine origin. All the types and symbols of the Old Testament, its sacrifices of cleansing and expiation, are impressive condemnations of sin and calls to repentance. The ever-ringing voices of prophecy are thrilling rebukes to wrong-doing and clarion appeals for righteousness. Its psalms and music are but echoing praise for the divine grace that renews the heart and restores the life to the blessedness of obedience to the moral laws of God. The lofty ethical demands of the Hebrew Scriptures, along with their revelation of grace, form a unique and distinguishing feature among ancient literatures. Their ceaseless voice is: "Keep judgment and do righteousness"; "Cease to do evil and learn to do well"; "Offer to God the sacrifices of righteousness." Nowhere else at that day was the moral ideal lifted so high, or with such imperative authority. The Old Testament ethics was a fit prophecy and preparation for the full Christian teaching. "If the ethics of the old dispensation had not passed into the fulfilment of the new, the Hebrew prophets and poets would still be the world's most inspiring teachers of high ethical hopes and ideals, and the moral code of Israel would be the school of righteousness, reverence, and law, to which the generations should go for the loftiest instruction."

The New Testament, which completes the authoritative records of Christianity, completes also Christianity's normative statement of the truths and principles of duty. These appear in the threefold form of (1) Christ's recorded teaching, (2) His personal example, and (3) the inspired interpretations of Christian duty in the apostolic writings. The teaching of Jesus, all through the gospels, while primarily religious and religiously spiritual, deals with the great realities of character and conduct, and, particularly in the Sermon on the Mount, ascends to the very heights and penetrates to the very depths of the laws of duty. It carries those laws into a spirituality, solemnity, and glory before unknown, and forms a representation which stands before the moral sense of the race as the unsurpassed and the unequalled ethical ideal. The view is carried up to the goal: "Be ye perfect, even as your Father in heaven is perfect." This divine teaching is at the same time reflected from the personal life of Christ. It is presented in living form. The example is part of the teaching—an example which is never lowered below the exalted range of the given precepts, and which has been instructing and inspiring all the centuries since. In the apostolic writings, under the guiding Spirit of truth, the teaching and pattern of Christ, together with his redemptive gospel, are applied to wide and varied ranges of practical life, the apostles themselves being filled with an ever-increasing appreciation of their divine import and transcendence. These inspired Scriptures, because of their unique and supreme authority for Christianity itself, are the fundamental and decisive standard of Christian ethics.

(2) But there is a secondary and auxiliary source for formulation of Christian ethics—in the Christian moral consciousness. In this, Christianity exhibits its moral principles and meaning as they enter into the inner experience of men, where they may be studied and estimated. Christianity is a "life," a "new life," in whose moral consciousness its principles and forces are acting formatively for character. Not only of "the life" that in Christ was "the light of men," but of all the pure life that is from him, is it true: "the life is the light of men." The ethicized Christian consciousness reveals the principles and laws that have come into it. It is a maxim in theology that only the regenerated and sanctified mind has a clear interpretative insight into spiritual truth, and can form the true theologian. The maxim holds, just as truly, with respect to moral truth. The spiritual and moral are inseparably united, and no man can judge with unhindered and reliable discrimination in matters of Christian ethics whose heart is unsympathetic or averse to the duties of the Christian life. The light shines in the darkness, but the darkness comprehends it not. Christian ethics, therefore, in formulating its ideas and completing its theoretical view rightly, draws upon the Christian consciousness, as that consciousness is scripturally determined, and interprets, not the Scriptures alone, but also, in auxiliary relation, the ethicized life of Christian humanity. While, therefore, it is the science of Biblical morality, it is also of the whole moral development of Christianized life, both in personal consciousness and in the observed historical fruitage of Scripture doctrine.

4. It is necessary to look at some of the particular elements or features of the clearer and fuller ethical view which comes from these sources.

Duties made More Definite

(1) Most of the duties naturally discerned by the conscience from the known relations of life are brought into more distinct and definite view by Christian revelation and experience. The natural discernment is often unclear, uncertain, partial, and faulty. The blindness, mistakes and misgivings of the moral sense form a large and perplexing chapter in the story of non-Christian morality. It has often led to doubt whether there is such a thing as a fixed, sure, immutable morality. A remedy for this has been needed. By its immense number of specific *precepts* for particular relations and circumstances, revelation gives correctness, minuteness, and fullness of application to the general principles of duty asserted by the moral sense. In manifold cases the conscience would be in the dark, or have only obscure or partial view, without the instruction and guidance thus supplied. Scarcely a situation or emergency in life can be named for which precept and counsel have not been given. When the sun rises the eye sees not only farther, but more minutely and with more certainty. Myriads of objects and relations before unseen flash into view. So by the light of the Scriptures, more of duty is known and better known. By common consent, even among skeptics as to the Christian religion, the ethical precepts of Christianity, in their purity and elevation, in their quickening directness and radical thoroughness, in their explicitness and universality, form an aggregate moral directory unapproached by the best codes of pagan sages or human philosophies, and add a grand aid to the moral judgments.

Human Relations

(2) The human *relations*, on which duty rests, have been brought into broader and fuller view by Christian teaching. Much of the disability, under which morality has suffered, has always come from a faulty understanding, if not total ignorance, of the varied relations which are to be filled out with their exact and full measure of duty. The idea of God and man's relation to him has often been falsely or misleadingly conceived. The history of

thought as to inter-human relations, from the closest to the most extended, presents a sad story of misapprehension, error, ignorance and consequent wrong. When these great vital relations are themselves misconceived, looked at from a false or obscuring view-point, one of the prime conditions for correct moral judgments is absent. Positive misdirection is in play. When our knowledge has not yet shown us clearly man's place in God's plan of the world, or the adaptations and purposes in human nature itself; when neither the great fact of personality nor that of human solidarity is correctly understood, as for example, when the individual is reduced, as has often been the case, to mere material for the state or for possible enslavement by captors, or he is, on the other hand, looked upon as an isolated and unrelated unit; or when the reality and meaning of the universal brotherhood of man, under the universal fatherhood of God, is not seen, the duties and obligations of life must necessarily be much obscured and unperceived.

But here the Christian revelation comes in with one of its great forms of help—a divine disclosure of our moral relations. It reveals some otherwise undiscoverable relations, opening to view additional obligations and responsibilities. It sets before us our solemn relations to God, to his renewing and saving grace, as well as to his creating and preserving love, to offered blessings, gracious rewards, and eternal destinies. The whole horizon of life is lifted and broadened, and the sphere of the moral activity and consequences extends into a future life. Man becomes a child of immortality and his home is eternity. The world and human life have a grandly changed meaning under the gospel. Man's place in the system of things, as to the past, present, and future is revealed in a light increased and broadened like that on the landscape when morning rises upon night; and in this light he sees a thousand new responsibilities on which he is touching every moment, and which stretch out and on in illimitable ranges. Conscience is enabled to act in view of all these new relations as well as the irradiated old ones, and taught to hold the heart and life, the will and activities to the moral requirements of this enlarged and illuminated ethical domain.

Moral Duties Divine Obligations

(3) Christian teaching has elevated the ethical view in closely uniting all moral obligation with duty to God. Natural ethics, when its implications are rationally followed up, is, indeed, theistic, and finds the seat of moral law in God as the absolute ground of the whole moral constitution. But from this movement, rising from the law of right in the conscience and in the moral constitution of the world, such ethics has yet this limitation, that duty is thought of from the human side, and not from the standpoint of God, who in his personal nature and will is both the source and goal of moral law. In this mode of forming the theory God is apt to be left remote, virtue is abstractly conceived and remains a reality too much by itself and separated from any enforcing or helping authority. It becomes too abstract and simply humanistic. But our view of moral good must be lifted into closer and more living connection with God. And so, Christianity, to transfuse the ethical sense with religions light and motives, teaches us to look upon right and duty from the standpoint of God. This is in accordance with the very design of Christianity as a redemptive and saving religion, seeking to bring man into true and practical fellowship with God. The moral discernment is to be filled and animated by the religious spirit, so that the moral training may be carried on and completed together with the development and consummation of the Christian life. Thus the form of the appeal is: "Be ye holy, for I am holy." "Be ye perfect, even as your Father in heaven is perfect." In a high and peculiar emphasis all duty is required to be done as unto God. "Forasmuch as ye have done it to the least of these, ye have done it unto me." "We should so fear and love God," as not to offend against any part of the law or fail in doing good. Through the Christian revelation alone the ethical conception and relation of God is truly attained, and with it a right conception of man and the highest spirit of duty.

In thus teaching that all duties should be fulfilled as something due to God, and under inspiration of love to Him, Christian ethics is not to be understood to mean that rational ethical theory is mistaken when it claims that men are to "do right because it is right." But it means to remind us where alone the absolute right is found—only in God. And it means that both the religious and the ethical life is to upraise and anchor us to Him, and to eternal righteousness as it is in Him. All duty is owed finally to God, because He is the one absolute righteous Being to whom the whole universe owes its very existence and all its blessings. Thus Christian ethics sets forth fully what rational thought has often caught a glimpse of and hinted at, but wanted vision to see clearly, viz.: that the goal of the ethical aim is to be "like God." Its aim, as is that of religion itself, is to bring our moral life into living fellowship with Him and His blessedness. This marked feature of Christian teaching presents the ethical view in its highest elevation, purification and power.

Moral Guilt

(4) In harmony with this close connection of the moral with the religious life, a further special feature of Christian ethics is a peculiar emphasis upon the guilt of offense against the moral law. In pagan ethics, often with no clear perception of the existence of God, always without just conception of his character, though the moral distinction was recognized and wrong was regarded as consumable, yet because the wrong was viewed as traversing only an abstract principle or an accredited usage or order of best happiness, it evoked no strong sense of guilt. Right was always little else than a conforming of one's self to "nature," or "reason," or "civil authority," or conditions of "well-being" or "enjoyment," or at best to an ideal conception of virtue. In the ethical view which materialistic philosophies present, though the phenomenon of conscience is acknowledged and obedience to its direction admitted to be necessary for proper right order, yet the condemnatory judgment on immorality is rather a judgment of it as unwise, imprudent, and injurious than as guilty and worthy of punishment. It is at most a non-conformity to an impersonal, mechanically determined, ongoing nature. The whole utilitarian conception of morality, which makes it consist essentially in following the teachings of experience as to what is most advantageous and useful, may hold disregard of it as a great

"evil," economically viewed, but almost annuls, if it does not completely remove, the idea of guilt, by substituting that of loss. Even in simply rational *theistic* ethics, despite theistic presuppositions and conclusions, the view may still deal too much with abstractions and rest too much on abstract ideas or impersonal things. Right and wrong are, indeed, developed by natural relations, to which men are bound to conform, but only because these relations, by being divinely established, represent God, who in the perfections of his nature and will, is at once the free Creator and righteous personal Ruler of the universe. Moral law not only applies alone to free personality, but has its source and authority in the Absolute Personality whose holy and beneficent will has constituted the moral relations and requirements of life. Morality pertains, not to the relations of mere things to things, or of persons to simply impersonal nature, but of persons to persons. Inter-human relations create and exhibit obligations because God's plan and will speak in them, but the full solemnity of moral obligation appears only when all inter-human obligations are seen carried up and united in the supreme and all-embracing obligation to God, to whom all duty is due. When these inter-human duties are refused, they are refused to God who requires them and has expressed that requirement to reason through the relations themselves and through his word. Not only the religious duties, as faith and love and gratitude and prayer, but all human duties are owed to Him. Here all religious duties become moral obligations; and all moral obligations become religious duties. And the guilt of wrong-doing is heightened by the fact that it is a sin against the just, holy, supreme authority and will of God, the absolute personal ground of the right order and blessedness of the universe. In Him the moral authority is identified with the rights of the Creator to whom every good in the universe is owed. This emphasis upon the transcendent authority and sanctity of moral law and consequent guilt of its violation is a special feature in the Christian ethical view and necessary for the true force and efficiency of the moral sense.

Any separation of morality from the position of something due to God personally, obscures and weakens the ethical view.

This has been the bane not only of pagan, materialistic, atheistic, or grossly utilitarian theories, but also of many other forms of representation. Whenever the sense of duty is resolved into an instinct, or blind feeling, or sympathy, or a product of custom, its true authority is kept out of sight. The guilt of neglect of it disappears. Though fervently regarded by many great thinkers as a sublime statement of the moral principle, even the Kantian "categorical imperative," an immediate behest of the reason, saying: "Do this, or do that," giving no account of itself or ground for its authority, but speaking autocratically in its own right, and as sufficient and final in its own imperative, under the abstract rule: "Act as if the maxims of thy action were to become by thy will the law of the universe," holds the whole moral authority too abstractly and remote from God for complete theory or effective power. He is not brought clearly into view or made livingly near, but left in the background—a Being whose existence, along with freedom and immortality, is only inferred and to be believed because this ideal "law" requires Him for its maintenance. Sublime as the "categorical imperative" may often have seemed, this shaping of the theory of obligation is not suited to fill and vivify the moral consciousness of men as does a sense of the sublimer reality of the holy will and supreme authority of God, as present in and speaking through that moral consciousness. But the Christian view brings us face to face with this righteous will and authority in every moral obligation, and teaches us to see in all the established personal relations of life a divine call to right and duty.

Moral Law Universal

(5) The Christian view makes uniquely clear the universalism of the moral law. In natural theories the reach and identity of the law has Moral Law failed rightly to appear. The theory has formed only an ethics for a race, a nation, a condition or caste. It has been particularistic, limited by race lines, tribal or national boundaries, class distinctions, or ancestral traditions. Codes of duty have been shaped to local and exclusive conditions. So we have a national ethics created by civil law, or a class ethics, as of

free citizens contra-distinguished from slaves, or of Brahmans as different from low caste people. Or we have an ethics of individuals, in which the code of duty of each is determined by his own personal "instincts," "feelings," swing of "sympathy," preference in "pleasure," development of "reason," calculations of "utility," ancestral "inheritance," or a mysterious "categorical imperative." Moral codes have been immensely and confusingly diversified. A self-identical and common standard does not appear, nor the clear, sure foundation of any. The moral law is not exhibited in its universality and permanence. Its grandeur is unseen by reason of the kaleidoscopic variations presented by the moving fragmentary theories. Its authority is brought into doubt. The great want has been a view of morality for man as man, authoritative everywhere and always, co-extensive with humanity.

The defect of the theories has been twofold. 1. They have not brought the whole race of man together in the essential sameness of a universal humanity, each individual being endowed with the high attributes of a personality, made in the image of God, and all bound together in one all-inclusive brotherhood. 2. They have failed clearly to unite this total humanity, in all its personalities, with God, whose nature and will is the only and absolute source of the moral law which sweeps round and through all the world. The Christian Scriptures and the Christian consciousness supply the needed completion of view by throwing both these truths into clear light. Christianity invests human personality with a worth, sacredness, and responsibility never else-where recognized. It is at the point of personality that each individual is to be united in fellowship with the personal God, who, as righteousness and love, sits, upon the throne. Christianity seeks to make so real and living the brotherhood of man, that the throb of love and sympathy may be felt across all national lines and race distinctions around the earth. And while it thus strengthens the vitality and sacred force of the relations that thus bind men together, it teaches that the moral duties to men which these relations require, are to be done as unto God. Monotheism brings *mono-nomism.* The moral law, which is absolute, self-identical, eternal and immutable in the holy nature and will of God, becomes universal and irrepealable not only for the earth but for all the moral universe.

Condition of Fulfillment

(6) A special extension in the Christian ethical view is the truth that the moral law can be truly fulfilled only in and through a spiritual regeneration and renovation of the personal life. This is a truth which simply rational theories fail to formulate, though they are not without materials to justify the formulation of it. Few facts of life and history are more conspicuous than the impotence of the ethical perceptions and motives to get and maintain rightful rulership. Some hindering and disabling depravity in the human condition prevents attainment of the moral ideal. Apart from the dreadful sway of vice and crime and cruel wrong, even with the well-disposed, full duty to neither God nor man is completely realized. The words put by Ovid in the mouth of Medea: *"Video meliora, proboque, detereora sequor"* (I see and approve the better, I follow the worse), voice the moral weakness felt even in pagan consciousness. This incompetency of the ethical behests to accomplish the true and required life, Christianity confirms and emphasizes; and upon its basis unfolds the necessity of a deep, radical renewal of personal character.

In Christianity, let it be remembered, the moral law is a diviner and deeper reality than natural notions of men make it. It looks, with its divine eye, down into the very depths of the heart, and demands loyal and full duty through the whole range of personal relations with respect to both God and man. It spreads the force of moral obligation over religious duties, joining them in indissoluble union. "The law of the Lord is perfect," and requires this wholeness of duty and righteousness. Hence Christianity holds a merely natural morality always to be faulty, leaving men under the law's condemnation. Without a divine quickening and spiritual enabling, men can never be brought to true and full obedience and transformed into moral harmony and likeness with God. And the proclamation, looking to this part of the redemptive process, is: "Except a man be born again he cannot see the kingdom of God." Thus it becomes a unique distinction of the Christian ethical view, that it proposes to bring men to spiritual and moral endeavor and victory from the starting-point of a conviction and recognition of their own thorough incompetence for the moral task. It furnishes a true and adequate ability where it has broken up dependence on an insufficient one.

But this brings to us the moral task, which belongs to the next chapter.

CHAPTER XII

THE ETHICAL TASK UNDER CHRISTIANITY

The ethical task is to fulfil the moral law, to actualize the ethical ideal in conduct and character. It is to turn obligations into life. It is not enough to know duty, even in completest theory. It must be realized. In its most important and final view, ethics is a question of moral power.

The impotence of the conscience before the moral task has always been an impressive fact. The perception of duty has lacked efficiency for the enforcement of duty. Vision of the right largely fails to secure conformity to it. Even the clearest intellectual discriminations and illuminations of the moral law have often been only as the play of cold light, almost like the aurora of the north quickening nothing into life or fruitage. Here is found the chief point of failure in natural ethics. It has power to dictate, but not to move. It wants an efficient dynamic for overcoming the moral evil that has established itself in human nature and life—evil so positive and dominant as to justify an apostle in representing the better ethical will as disabled: "Ye cannot do the things that ye would." Prof. Flint says: "The wisdom of the heathen world, at its very best, was utterly inadequate to the accomplishment of such a task as creating a due abhorrence of sin, controlling the passions, purifying the heart, and ennobling the conduct."

The aim of Christianity is supremely practical. It seeks to save from sin and bring to righteousness. It wastes no effort for simply speculative results. It comes "not in word only, but in power." Besides its service to morals in confirming and extending our needed knowledge of duty, its greatest ethical service is in supplying the needed dynamic or efficacious force for the realization of the holy life. How does it enable the moral task?

Completion of the Ethical View

1. In some degree by the completion of the ethical view itself. The clearer light is forceful and efficacious for a better realization of the moral task. "Knowledge is power," especially knowledge which throws into view the most impressive realities and relations, and appeals with the most cogent motives. By the strong illumination shed upon the general principles of right and virtue, by the definiteness and detail of the instruction and precepts for all situations in life, by the elevation of view in which the moral horizon is widened and extended, so as to show a living brotherhood of every man with every other round the world and a range of moral interests and responsibilities interminable as eternity, by the emphasis with which men are made amenable to God for all moral duties, even those to men, thus vivifying the whole moral consciousness with a sense of a close, unescapable accountability to God the conscience is better enlightened and quickened for its task, strengthened by the fullest certainty and under the vigor of a new inspiration. It has more light for direction; it bears grander motive forces before the will.

Assurance of Success

2. By giving assurance of success. In the face of the greatest hindrances and natural incompetence, it certifies an inspiring goal of the moral endeavor. Pointing to redemptive grace, it makes manifest that the administration of this world is not on the side of moral evil, or indifferent to its wrong and blight, but is working for its overthrow, the deliverance of its subjects, and their triumph over it. It proclaims an established and ever-advancing "kingdom," whose consummation will bring all those who, as its subjects, "hunger and thirst after righteousness," triumphantly through and beyond the present militant stage of

the moral life into final victory over evil, "a new earth and a new heaven wherein dwelleth righteousness." In this divine assurance that the domination of moral evil, with its anarchy and misery in the soul, is no necessity, that its overthrow is provided for, and that God's government is so in the interest of righteousness and love as to guarantee victory to even the feeblest that in faith appropriate his grace and help, there comes the full inspiration, not only of hope. but of sure success in the moral endeavor. Moral effort is not compelled to be

"Like ships that sailed for sunny isles,
But never came to shore."

It has the certainty that

"To him who sides with god
No chance is lost."

The moral help thus supplied by Christianity is well illustrated by the contrast which it presents to some other teaching, say as seen in Buddhism, extolled in poetry as "The Light of Asia." This is known as one of "the great religions." It is, rather, a philosophy of life, a directory for conduct. It is an atheistic, or at best a pantheistic philosophy, recognizing no personal God and emptying the idea of Deity of practical validity. It had its origin in a deep and oppressive sense of the evil and misery of life, and aimed at their solution and the way of deliverance. On the basis of the oriental "metempsychosis," with its supposed perpetual re-births, on account of earlier sins, into successive distressful lives, it elaborated, for deliverance, a code of duty pervaded by the ascetic spirit and demanding the severest self-discipline. In many of its separate precepts it rises, indeed, here and there to elevations and beauties of moral idea that seem almost akin to the finest and purest of New Testament inculcations. But whether viewed as a philosophy or a religion Buddhism has no personal God, who loves and values men as his own children made in his own image, and ready to come to their help. It has heard, and in its atheistic cosmos, can hear, no voice of redemption, knows of no manifestation of a loving God for deliverance of his sinful children from their sins and their exaltation to the dignity and happiness of fellowship with Himself. In this despair of help from God, in this dolefully pessimistic view of the world and life, and driven to depend only on self-help, is it any wonder that the moral task is directed, not to the development, elevation and joy of personal life, but to its repression, subjugation, and reduction, so as to bring it, at its earthly close, to Nirvana, extinction of conscious individual existence, as the greatest good! By as much as this theory of despair is suited to atrophy all nerve for the ethical task, and sink personality from its true intended elevation of divine fellowship and excellence into the inanity of unconscious being, by so much does the Christian truth of the assured success and victory of right and goodness in the advancing kingdom of God's grace and eternal love, exalting the worth and force of personality to the highest, inspire and sustain the moral endeavor. "Forasmuch as ye know that your labor is not in vain in the Lord."

Much has been written in late years about "the evolution of the moral life," by writers who seek to account for it through the action of merely naturalistic forces in the human constitution and in its physical environment. The above contrast is suggestive of factors in the problem which many of these writers overlook.

Religious Interest

3. By uniting the moral side of life with the religious, and so bringing all the powers of the religious interest in vital help for the moral task. The common false disruption between morality and religion, classifying duties to God as religious, and only duties to fellow-men or self as moral, each standing in isolation, and largely of separate accomplishment, allowing men to be "moral" while repudiating all their duties to God, or "religious" while without a conscience enforcing duty to men, leaves flabby nerve for moral endeavor. All the mighty motives from the Godward side are lost. No quickening force for inter-human duties comes from a consciousness of God and his authority, or the future life. Any view that severs morality from God and is bounded by this world and temporal good, must fail to realize the

moral life of man. But the Christian view allows no such separation. It unites the two as two sides of the same life of duty, out of one conscience, with vision of both God and men, and one heart true to the indivisible spirit of right. As religious duties are all moral, as obligations to God, and all moral duties are religious, as due to Him, the Christian consciousness of God must reinforce and vivify with new efficiency the whole twofold moral endeavor. All the distinctly religious interests and forces, reverence of Deity, repentance before God, gratitude, faith, love, hope, spiritual joy, aspiration, desire of immortality and endless blessedness, thus brought into concurrent action with the Christianly enlightened natural conscience, bring an immensely advantageous condition for the actualization of the ethical life. "To believe in an ever-living and perfect Mind, supreme over the universe, is to invest moral distinctions with immensity and eternity, and lift them from the provincial stage of human society to the imperishable theatre of all being. When planted thus in the very substance of things, they justify and support the ideal estimates of the conscience; they deepen every guilty shame; they guarantee every righteous hope; and they help the will with a Divine casting-vote in every balance of temptation."

Power of Holy Spirit

4. By the enlightening and obligating force of the Holy Spirit. This reality is assured both in the teaching of the Scriptures and the testimony of the Christian consciousness. We must distinguish between the simply natural action of conscience and the quickening and helping by the divine Spirit. Revelation fully recognizes the natural conscience and its obligating energy, Rom. 2:15; 1:20. It designates it by the term συνείδησις from σύνοιδα, *conscius sum*—a knowing with, *i. e.* a conjoined consciousness of self and of right, or a knowing with God, whose law it discerns. Its natural functions of discernment and imperative are not set aside by the Spirit, but enlightened and re-in-forced. His part must not be counted zero. "When the Spirit is come, He will convince the world of sin, of righteousness, and of judgment," John 16:8. He works through the truth, in and through men's

natural faculties. While the Christian's own conscience is acting in its natural functions, it is not acting alone. It is not alone; for the Holy Spirit is there as a quickening and helping power. In this is fulfilled the experience expressed by St. Paul: "My conscience also bearing me witness in the Holy Ghost," Rom. 9:1. This is a Christian conscience, one acting not alone and unaided, but embraced within and filled by the influence of the Holy Spirit. This influence has been well expressed as "like the energy of the sun shine in the fruit."

Spiritual Regeneration

5. Through spiritual regeneration and renovation. It is through this profound reality that Christianity accomplishes its great ethical result. It places the principle of holiness, of duty to God and men, in the very heart of human nature and life. It writes the law in the love of the soul.

The divine wisdom of Christianity is marked by the stress which it places upon a purification of the inner life, "the heart," the very fountain of thought, purpose, and conduct. It points to the immoral source of the immoralities of conduct: "Out of the heart proceed murders, adulteries," etc. The remedy must purify the fountain. When this is secured and the law of holiness is established there, the ethical life, in its manifoldness and many-sidedness, comes into realization.

It is thus that the conscience gains control. Its failures result from the strength of opposing passions, desires, and perverted inclination, excited often by temptations without. The affections do not find their center and rest in God and righteousness. They are irregular, often sordid and misleading. The appetites and passions obscure the moral discernments and resist the moral judgments. There is a law of "sin in the members." The will, which should bow to the direction of the conscience, is swayed by wrong motives. The scepter of the moral faculty is broken by the rebellion of desires at war with right and duty. The faintest whisper of conscience ought to be decisive, but against the imperious ascendency of wrong affections its loudest imperatives prove impotent. But in this moral renovation, giving its "new heart and right spirit," the affections come into harmony with God and all that is good. It is the "writing of the law again in the heart," in the understanding and love. To this new life in the affections, duty becomes a pleasure. The conscience, no longer perplexed and overborne by evil desires, becomes able to assert its rightful authority. The will attains its rightful freedom and power to control efficiently in the domain of righteousness, and to hold the life in the harmonies of right and duty.

Put these different elements of the Christian ethical dynamic together. They aggregate the final moral power. Christianity completes the ethical view, flooding all the principles of right and duty with impressive light. It throws broad and strong illumination over all the moral relations of men, extending the view into the future life, and giving certifying precepts for guidance and support. It gives the inspiring assurance of the triumph of righteousness in the kingdom which God's love is establishing for it. It unites all moral duties under the sanctions and solemnities of obligation to God, and reinforces them by all the motives and appeals which the religious sentiments and interests address to men. It supplies an exhaustless wealth of truths which give nerve to moral endeavor and are directly convertible into character. And, as expressing the line along which these elements all pass into full effect, by its regenerative action it secures for the innermost sources of conduct a transforming influence which does for the life what making the tree good does for its fruit. Love of right turns convictions of right into character. The efficiency of the conscience no longer stands only in the intellectual judgments, but also in affection for the morally good. With love toward what is good a feebler conscience could sway the life aright. But under this deep inward change, we have clearer moral vision and stronger imperative, together with a transformation of the whole nature into predominant love of righteousness. As the Christian life advances, the principles of duty are more and more established in the heart and conduct as life-forces, and the conscience becomes more and more *de facto*, as it is *de jure*, sovereign for moral obedience. And thus Christianity supplies the divine and sufficient dynamic for the full realization of the ethical life.

www.ingramcontent.com/pod-product-compliance
Lightning Source LLC
LaVergne TN
LVHW051122080426
835510LV00018B/2190